St. John's, Newfoundland, *Evening Mercury* established.

Ernest Thompson Seton appointed Official Naturalist for Manitoba.

Canadian Rugby Union formed.

Gas lighting introduced in Winnipeg.

G. M. Grant publishes *Picturesque Canada*.

1883

Marquis of Lansdowne becomes governor general of Canada (1883-1888).

Amalgamation of the Grand Trunk and Great Western Railways.

Canada Southern Railway completes bridge at Niagara.

Construction in St. John's, Newfoundland, of dry-dock 600 feet long, 132 feet wide, large enough to take the largest ship afloat.

Methodist churches in Canada unite.

Beginning of the work of the Salvation Army in Canada.

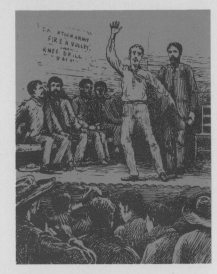

Valuable nickel-copper deposits are discovered near Sudbury during construction of the CPR.

Regina *Leader* established by Nicholas Flood Davin.

The *Week* established in Toronto by Goldwin Smith.

Canada adopts Sandford Fleming's system of standard time.

Thirteen salmon canneries, operating on the Fraser River in B.C., produce 199,000 cases.

First public library in Ontario opens at Guelph.

Abbé Casgrain publishes the *Oeuvres complètes* of Octave Crémazie.

Farmers union meets at Winnipeg; drafts a bill of rights; sends a delegation to Ottawa.

Montreal holds first winter carnival.

Robert Harris commissioned to paint *The Fathers of Confederation*.

Toronto Trades Assembly begins organization of the Trades and Labor Congress. Included assemblies of the Knights of Labor.

1884

Louis Riel returns to Canada from exile in U.S.

Calgary Agricultural Society, forerunner of Calgary Stampede, organized.

Canadian voyageurs, comm... by General Wolseley, man t... expedition up the Nile to res... General Gordon at Khartou...

...along Lower St. Lawrence.

Montreal's *La Presse* established.

Isabella Valancy Crawford publishes *Old Spookses' Pass, Malcolm's Katie and Other Poems* at her own expense.

Free public library established in Toronto.

...an Athletic Union of ...nada formed.

Humber railway collision near Toronto; 31 lives lost.

First salmon hatchery constructed on Fraser River, B.C.

Date Due

APR 2 3 1978		
MAY 1 2 1978	JUN 2 6 1990 SEP 2 8 1992	
NOV 3 - 1978	OCT 1 3 1992	
NOV 2 4 1978	DEC 1 7 1998 JUN 1 7 2004	
JUN 9 1979		
OCT 2 0 1979		
JAN 1 3 1984		

CANADA MOVES WESTWARD

More to follow

CALGARY HOUSE

My Carter

A squa[w]...

Proving the ford

At High River

A Squatter

John Swain Eng.

Il n'a quarante deux années passées que je n'ai pas m Québec!

Crossing Sheep Cr[eek]

JACK BATTEN
CANADA MOVES WESTWARD
1880/1890

Canada's Illustrated Heritage

Canada's Illustrated Heritage

Publisher: Jack McClelland
Editorial Consultant: Pierre Berton
Historical Consultant: Michael Bliss
Editor-in-Chief: Toivo Kiil
Associate Editors: Clare McKeon
Jean Stinson
Assistant Editors: Julie Dempsey
Marta Howard
Designer: David Shaw
Cover Artist: Alan Daniel
Picture Research: Lembi Buchanan
Michel Doyon
Judy Forman
Betty Gibson
Jonathan Hanna
Margo Sainsbury

ISBN: 0-9196-4420-1

N.S.L. Natural Science of Canada Limited
254 Bartley Drive
Toronto, Ontario M4A 1G4

Printed and bound in Canada

Jumbo, the elephant-wonder of P.T. Barnum's circus, was the most famous animal act of pre-motion picture days. Before the mighty beast was killed by a train in 1885 near St. Thomas, Ontario, business showmen like T. Eaton used him in their ads for dry goods.

Half-title: *"Sketches of British Columbia" from the* Illustrated London News, *March 10, 1883: "That extensive country is still awaiting development . . . Its future progress, however, will depend upon the eventual completion of the Canadian Pacific Railway."*

Title page: *John Swain, a traveller through Calgary and Fort Macleod in 1884, drew these vignettes of life in the Canadian West before the railway changed most aspects of daily life. The figure at centre is a Québecois cart driver; at top right, a squatter's family.*

CONTENTS

PROLOGUE   *A Typical Canadian Named P. Turner Bone* 6

ONE   *"We Are the Navvies"* 10

TWO   *The Mark of Good Breeding* 24

THREE   *A Voice to Every Cause* 36

FOUR   *The Curious Trail through Cannington Manor* 48

FIVE   *A Sorry Night in Chinatown* 58

SIX   *Campaign Clowns and Good London Gin* 68

SEVEN   *Drydock Days and Maritime Pride* 80

EIGHT   *"O Canada"* 92

NINE   *The Sons of Toil* 100

TEN   *That Colony – a Dangerous Nuisance* 112

Acknowledgements 124

Index 125

Picture Credits 128

Navvies and kitchen workers pose outside No. 1 shed at the Mackenzie and Holt Camp near Kicking Horse Pass, the section of the CPR construction where the narrator of our Prologue, "a typical Canadian named P. Turner Bone," worked for contractor Holt in the summer of 1884.

A TYPICAL CANADIAN NAMED P. TURNER BONE

Be Canadians and the future is yours.

Louis-Honoré Fréchette, 1887

"If the world lasts long enough," John J. Rowan allowed, speaking in 1881, "there is a glorious future in store for Canadians." John J. Rowan was not, of course, a Canadian himself. He was a well-to-do English sportsman-traveller who toured the Dominion in the early eighties and lent the natives his opinion of their promising land. But it's doubtful if many Canadians at the end of the decade would have echoed Rowan's glowing prediction, because the eighties were a confusing time, remarkable for giddy highs and terrible lows, spotted by depressions and spurts of prosperity, full of glorious accomplishments and of bitter outbursts of racial and religious bigotry.

Sir John A. Macdonald, who presided over Canada's government and set the style for its politics during the entire ten years, confidently proclaimed in 1881 that "the nation has come together to stay." But within the next few years two provinces elected premiers – Nova Scotia, William Fielding in 1884 and Quebec, Honoré Mercier in 1887 – who toyed with the idea of secession from Canada as the only solution to their provinces' woes.

In the same short span of ten years, Canadians organized a haven in Manitoba for Russian Jews fleeing the Czar's pogroms, but they indulged in a rage of rioting and murder to drive Chinese labourers away from their western shores. Between 1880 and 1890, the number of newspapers publishing in the country increased by 30 dailies, 167 weeklies and 61 monthlies; but when the Marquis of Lorne, Canada's governor general from 1878 to 1883, set about organizing a literary society of Canadian writers, he ran into sneers from all sides, especially from the press. "Nincompoops" was the Toronto *Globe's* description of the society's first members.

And throughout the eighties, Canadians could hardly decide which they revered more, liquor or religion. In Toronto, typically, the contest finished in a dead heat – the city boasted some seventy churches but there were at least as many saloons, and both institutions enjoyed flat-out capacity business. Parishioners attending the largest, most fashionable churches had to fight their way to their pews; the only ones assured of seats were the reporters who stationed themselves directly under the pulpit to record the minister's sermon for next day's papers. As for the bars, they conceded only Sunday to the churches, closing down each Saturday evening at a temperate 7:00 P.M. But they opened promptly at 6:00 A.M. the other days of the week to accommodate customers anxious for a shot before work.

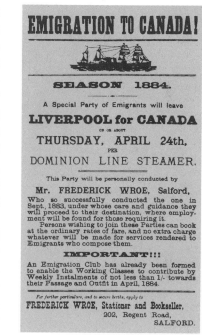

Between 1881 and 1891, nearly 900,000 immigrants found their way to Canada, mostly from Britain.

In a decade of such paradoxes, perhaps of all citizens, a modest, gritty young gentleman with the prosaic name of P. Turner Bone might exemplify Canada as worthily as any man. And perhaps much of the country's daily life and hard times might appear less confused, glanced at through his eyes. True, Turner Bone wasn't born a Canadian or even a North American; but he emigrated from Scotland in his early twenties, reaching his new homeland on February 6, 1882, on the bitter, blizzarding morning when the good ship *Peruvian* from the Allan Steamship Line put in to Halifax harbour.

an appropriate profession

Bone soon found that he had automatically joined a large, established body of Canadian citizens – the Scottish-born and Scottish-descended. There were 699,863 of them in 1881, an astonishing number occupying high places in Canadian commerce and industry, living in the austere mansions that had assumed a permanent role in the landscape along Sherbrooke Street in Montreal and Jarvis Street in Toronto. Thus, P. Turner Bone, unlike the bewildered Hungarians who blundered into settlement in southeastern Saskatchewan in the early eighties and unlike the Irish Catholics who huddled in a Montreal ghetto, felt immediately at home.

What's more, Bone was an engineer, trained in the Glasgow firm of Kyle, Denninson and Frew, and there was no more crucial or appropriate profession in the years when, at last, the building of the Canadian Pacific Railway was solidly underway. Bone, indeed, came armed with letters of introduction to two of an uncle's friends, R.B. Angus and Duncan McIntyre, old countrymen naturally, and both directors of the CPR at head office in Montreal.

Scottish, an engineer, young, a little blindly

drawn toward the wilderness, seeking to tame it with that great nineteenth-century civilizing instrument, the railroad – Bone seemed precisely equipped for Canada in the 1880s. And as he travelled across the country, he observed with affection and a certain cool awe the institutions, customs and pleasures, the men and the plans that were casting Canada into something he agreed was genuinely special.

Bone found himself an observer of many casually enlightening moments of Canadian life. He marvelled at the glory of the Montreal winter scene, packed with toboggan runs down city avenues, jingling with parades of ornate sleighs, tramped by hiking Snowshoe Club zealots; at Toronto's orderly streets and dignified factories and the rancorous relations between two of its daily papers, the *Mail* and the *Globe,* forever deploring one another's taste and policies; and at the hustling frontier ruggedness of Winnipeg in the throes of its high-flown, boom-town years.

adventure tales

Bone just happed to be lounging in a baked-dry Calgary street one sweltering August afternoon in 1883 when T.B. Braden came by hawking the very first issue of his and A.M. Armour's Calgary *Weekly Herald,* one of the pioneer prairie papers. And two years later when he was supervising some bridge construction on the final stages of the CPR through the Rockies, hundreds of militant rail workers rose up in a fury at the debt-plagued railroad's delays in paying salaries, closed down Bone's project and marched on the CPR offices in a strike movement that, for a few days, threatened to shut down the entire railway.

In the land boom that hit Calgary in the mid-1880s, Bone picked up two lots in a prime location at $450 for a corner lot, $300 for an inside lot. And in the summer of 1886 as he was tending

FROM HALIFAX TO VANCOUVER

Miss Canada: "This is what we want, Cousin Jonathan. It will give us real independence, and stop the foolish talk about annexation."

Jonathan: "Wal, Miss, I guess you're about right thar; but I'll believe it when I see it!"

to some repairs to the CPR line deep in the Rockies, who should coast by, seated on the cow-catcher of a train's locomotive, embarked on a first triumphant inspection tour? None other than the prime minister, Sir John A. "Facing the wind as he was," Turner Bone dutifully reported, "his eyelids kept up a continual blinking and it is doubtful if he was really enjoying his trip."

Bone was even privileged to enjoy a social evening presided over by that most famous and formidable sportsman, Ned Hanlan. Rowing still reigned as the nation's first mass spectator sport, almost entirely because Hanlan had established himself as the world's single unbeatable oarsman in the seventies. But he was just as renowned in his native Toronto as a convivial, hard-drinking host at his hotel on the lovely island in Toronto Bay. "Accompanied by Hanlan himself," Bone recorded, "we were taken to the Island in a steamer chartered for the occasion. He had the boat first circle the Island several times before landing us; and by that time we had got so twisted around that he didn't know where he was, nor did he recognize his own hotel when the boat drew up alongside the pier. It was a great night."

When Turner Bone headed west in the early summer of 1883, he was following the dreams of all Canadians who valued their country's destiny. The world depression in the seventies had temporarily stifled ambitions and dreams. Maritimers had begun to retreat into themselves, victimized by the collapse of their one sure money-maker, the sailing-ship industry. Steam and iron had stolen usefulness and profits from sail and wood. Québecois were grumbling over Ottawa's supposed denial of their full racial and religious privileges, and British Columbians were wondering out loud just exactly what their ten-year-old connection with the other provinces, thousands of empty miles to the east, could possibly mean in dollars-and-cents business.

But the country's people were truly united in one way in 1880 – in a vision of the new West. Disgruntled Easterners dreamed of it as a rich, reviving homeland for themselves or their sons. Businessmen looked to it as the next territory for a bonanza boom in real estate, and manufacturers rubbed their hands over it as a potential market for their products. Ottawa nurtured hopes of luring farmers and workers from Britain and Europe. All Canadians, in one way or another, saw something of their future in the West.

But first came the railroad, the Canadian Pacific Railway. And its construction became the epic event of the eighties. In that period when the country wobbled under its doubts, when even England's attitude reflected "indifference and superciliousness," Canadians mustered the brains and the manpower to build one of the world's magnificent railroads, the mighty CPR that spanned nearly the width of the continent. The railroad renewed the country's pride and offered it an instrument of unity. The rail work all across the country was harsh and dangerous but it yielded the country a treasure of adventure tales that moved directly into the history books.

The Sherbrooke Fair of '86 boasted the completion of the CPR with a display of imports and produce brought east via transcontinental.

CHAPTER ONE

"WE ARE THE NAVVIES"

All I have to say is that the work was well done in every way.

William Van Horne

Canadians, not excluding Sir John A. himself, suspected from the beginning that their country was too young, too inexperienced, not rich or populous enough to build the Canadian Pacific Railway from its own resources. Thus, in the early years of the 1880s they relied on steel supplies from Krupp's works in Germany, on ten thousand coolies from China, on American timber and British navvies, and on engineers from New York and Edinburgh. And they went begging loans on every one of the world's great financial markets.

But in the end, from the men and machines and money of a dozen foreign countries, something purely Canadian was forged. Partly out of desperation ("I feel like a man walking on the edge of a precipice," said George Stephen, the president of the CPR) partly out of determination ("My last ambition," said Prime Minister Macdonald at age 66, "is to see the CPR safe"), Canada alone brought the most essential ingredient of all to the task of construction – the vision, the mighty dream that one day a railroad from Montreal to Vancouver *would* stitch together the perplexing, giant, sprawling wilderness and isolation. And the vision triumphed.

"To have built that road," said William Van Horne, the man who came from Illinois to supervise the construction of the CPR and stayed on to preside over it, "would have made a Canadian out of the German Emperor." Under the power of the dream, the CPR became a Canadian accomplishment, exclusively and proudly, the most magnificent feat of the decade, perhaps the most magnificent in all the years of Canadian life, and the railroad, in its turn, changed the country and its people.

The railroad made land speculation the first Big Business on the prairies. The trick was to guess in advance the exact route the surveyors would choose, then buy up land in the vicinity for resale to new settlers at inflated prices. Inevitably, there was more than an educated guess involved in the profits piled up by syndicates like the one that, in the spring of 1882, purchased acres of Hudson's Bay Company reserve land at an unlikely spot in southern Saskatchewan called Pile of Bones. The area was flat and dry, without trees for shade or fuel, without water for refreshment, but it did have in its favour His Honour, Edgar Dewdney, lieutenant-governor of the North-West Territories, who just happened to be a leading member of the land-buying syndicate.

"Well, Gore, you have hit it off pretty nicely," Dewdney announced in late May 1882 to a settler named Tom Gore who had "squatted" on land in

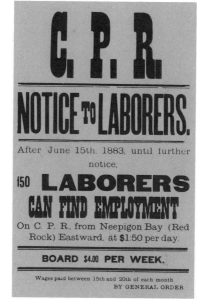

North of Superior, construction of the railway moved along quickly at first. Through the summer of 1883, seventy miles of track were laid from the Lakehead to Nepigon Bay.

***Opposite page**: The task of laying some of the most difficult track in B.C. fell to Andrew Onderdonk's men. Here one of his contractors takes a test ride in an inspection car built at the shops at Yale.*

John Macoun
Naturalist of the New West

The man who sold the CPR syndicate on the southern route for the railway was an enthusiastic, self-taught botanist named John Macoun. Born in Ireland in 1831, he emigrated to Canada as a young man, devoted himself to farming and the study of plants, and in 1868 was appointed professor at Albert College. In 1872 he accompanied Sandford Fleming on his western survey, and seven years later toured the southern prairies as a member of the Geological Survey. He returned East with optimistic reports of a fertile plain ideally suited for farming, debunking the drought-years observations of Hind and Palliser. The CPR immediately commissioned a southern survey of the eventual route, and the rest is history. Throughout the eighties, Macoun worked for the Survey, and in 1912 moved to B.C. where he died in 1920. He was the author of three books and many works on wildlife.

Pile of Bones. "It is just about here that the capital of the North-West Territories is likely to be located." And, sure enough, before the summer was out, dry, scrubby Pile of Bones was designated a CPR centre, named headquarters for the North-West Mounted Police and capital of the Territories, and assigned a more appropriately regal name – Regina.

In the end, Dewdney's syndicate made less money out of Regina than its members expected. They fell into a row with the other major land owner in the area, the CPR, whose officers retaliated by locating the station – which invariably became the rich business centre of any new prairie town – several blocks away from the syndicate's lots. Dewdney took the dispute to his friends in Ottawa who influenced the CPR to relocate the precious station closer to Dewdney's land, but in the wrangle the syndicate still lost its chance to milk the incoming settlers to quite the degree it had planned.

The ultimate route of the railroad killed the hopes and economies of scores of budding prairie towns in the early eighties. Rapid City, Dominion City, Mountain City, Crystal City – all of them flourished, at least in the dreams of settlers who invested in them in anticipation of the approaching railroad, and all faded as the CPR passed them by.

a thriving city appeared

For every town that the railway killed, it gave birth to half a dozen others. "Stores, hotels, dwelling-houses and other buildings were run up as if by magic," wrote botanist and surveyor John Macoun about Brandon in 1880, "and where nothing but prairie was seen in the spring the nucleus of a thriving city with all civilized appliances appeared before the short summer was passed." It was the railroad that made Brandon the commercial centre of western Manitoba, a town that by 1882 boasted a permanent population of 3,000 and twenty new hotels to accommodate the transient population of settlers and speculators heading west.

In the same way, two years later in 1884, Calgary blossomed with the arrival of the tracks into a town with a population of 506, with a Hudson's Bay store, three blacksmiths (all named John), the magnificent Calgary Bath House and Barber Shop, Dr. Henderson's Medical Hall and Cornelius J. Soule's photo studio (formal portraits, $1). Thanks to the CPR, business in Calgary hit inflationary peaks. "Had two pieces of repairing," George Murdock, harness maker, confided to his diary. "Charged like the mischief, as a dollar here is handled like 25¢ at home."

eager young pioneers

The most spectacularly mushrooming new prairie city was Winnipeg. In five meteoric years, between 1880 and 1886, it burst from an isolated town into a bustling metropolis of 20,000. It survived the inevitable collapse of the early land boom, a period when, in John Macoun's words, "real estate agents became as numerous as sands on the sea shore," and emerged as the railroad's true "doorway to the west," the supply centre for all arriving settlers.

The Pembina branch of the railroad, running from Winnipeg to the border where it linked up with an American line, had been operating since late 1879. In March 1882, the first train on the main CPR line from Fort William rolled into Winnipeg, dumping the first load of eager young pioneers to hit the city that year. To accommodate them, building contractors threw up clusters of homely, tar-papered shanties that, in one disgusted arrival's phrase, resembled "so many ugly black mushrooms."

Almost everything else in Winnipeg smacked

of the same hasty, make-shift ways. Mud oozed between the cracks in the plank sidewalks; the rough cedar blocks of the magnificently wide (132 feet at many points) Main Street echoed and banged in the traffic; all the streets teemed with crude, smelly ox-carts; and in the winter the city reverberated with the racket of dog trains.

For all its spiralling growth, Winnipeg still radiated a primitive, frontier atmosphere. Its population was aggressively masculine – for every woman, there were two men, most of them young bachelors scrambling for a stake in the new West. By night, liquor flowed like water in Carey's Grog Shop or in the Pacific and Queen's Hotels. The saloons and hotel beverage rooms weren't merely places for carousing; during the land boom, they also functioned as informal and rancorous offices for gaudy deals in real estate.

By 1886, Winnipeg's downtown streets were lined with no less than 88 wholesale houses handling a grand total of $15 million worth of business in everything from Red Fife wheat and the fancy new Massey Harvesters to Presbyterian hymnals.

gentility crept in

As the decade wore on, notes of permanent gentility crept into Winnipeg life – the railroad *did* introduce civilizing influences too. In 1885, the Hudson's Bay store, which occupied a handsome building on Main Street, began advertising "the most recent in Paris and London fashions imported by sea and rail." By the same year the Leland Hotel had acquired a reputation among experienced travellers as the West's pre-eminently refined stopping place.

The Manitoba Club, an organization 150 strong of the city's worthiest business leaders, confidently erected fine new quarters on Garry Street at the astronomical cost of $20,000, furniture included. The Odd Fellows, the Foresters, the

When Edgar Dewdney chose Pile of Bones as the site for the future capital of the N.W.T. in 1882, Westerners were outraged by the Lt.-Gov.'s conflict of interest in land speculation.

CALGARY: A TOWN IS BORN

The choice of a southern route for the CPR crushed the hopes of land agents and settlers in towns like Prince Albert, Battleford and Emerson while towns on the newly laid track boomed. Calgary was one of those towns. Founded in 1875 as a N.W.M.P. fort, by 1885 a mile of hotels and stores, saloons and livery stables lined Atlantic (9th) Ave. (right). By 1889 its population numbered over 2,500 (below).

Orange Order and Free Masons, the St. George, St. Andrew and St. Patrick Societies were all going strong by 1885, and John Macoun declared that his fellow Winnipeggers of the eighties "comprised a soundly church-going community. . . . On the Sabbath morn, except when the bells in the church towers call the citizens forth to worship, the streets are hushed and still." The good people of the city were certainly a stoutly independent lot: when City Council looked back over its spending for the year 1882, it discovered to its everlasting pride that it had handed out a mere $150, all told, to Winnipeg's charity cases.

working around the clock

The most important visitor to Winnipeg in any month of the early 1880s was a man forever in a desperate rush – William Van Horne, the whirlwind executive hired to guarantee the railroad's construction, quickly. "Van Horne sent for me in Winnipeg [in the late winter of 1882]," reported J.H.E. Secretan, a senior CPR surveyor, "and announced in a most autocratic manner that he wanted 'the shortest possible commercial line' between Winnipeg and Vancouver, also that he intended to build five hundred miles that summer. If I could show him the road, that was all he wanted, and if I couldn't, he would have my scalp."

Van Horne threw 5,000 men and 1,700 teams of horses on to the prairies. Frequently working shifts around the clock, the men laid 417 miles of track on the main line through Manitoba and the Territories and another 113 miles of spur tracks in the summer of 1882. The following year, they reached to within a few miles of Calgary, and in 1884 they began the tortuous cut through Kicking Horse Pass, a task that consumed two working seasons and another 5,000 labourers.

Van Horne's driving wrath wasn't the only burden the rail workers endured. They were tested by the isolation, by sudden prairie fires and by the West's eccentric weather. Turner Bone reported that, one spring day in the foothills of the Rockies, to his astonishment, his nose froze.

The Plains Indians whose concern grew as the line pierced into the Territories, were regarded as a threat by Van Horne who called on the Mounties to stand armed guard over his workers night and day. Father Albert Lacombe helped allay the fears of Indian violence. When the young warriors of the Blackfoot armed themselves to resist the railroad gangs' encroachments on their reserve lands west of Medicine Hat, Father Lacombe conferred with Chief Crowfoot over tea and tobacco for hour after tense hour, with Mounties and Indians standing by, bristling at one another. At the end of this most crucial tea party, he persuaded Crowfoot to call off his warriors. The railroad moved unhindered across the reserves, and Van Horne rewarded Father Lacombe with a free lifetime pass on any CPR train.

"quite impracticable"

The perils of track-laying in the Territories could not match the sheer hopelessness of the work through the Canadian Shield north of Lake Superior. One part muskeg to two parts rock, this area was, in the baleful opinion of surveyor J.H. Rowan, "quite impracticable for a railroad." "There is a gloominess about the surroundings," wrote Stuart Cumberland, an Australian journalist travelling through Northern Ontario, "which gives the onlooker the impression that Nature had been troubled with a fit of the blues when she created them."

Nevertheless, Van Horne attacked the Shield with 10,000 labourers and spent up to $300,000 per mile of track. He imported the first track-laying machine ever seen in Canada; he opened rock

Crowfoot
Chieftain of Peace

He was a veteran of arbitration. A distinguished warrior in his youth, he had succeeded Three Suns as chief of the Blackfoot in 1869 at age 33, and had counselled peace through the restive years of the '70s. He had been a powerful and wealthy man: he owned 400 horses, paid several aides, and had ten wives. He worked with missionaries and Mounties, trying to guide his people into a new way of life now that the buffalo were gone. But his health and influence were waning. Starvation was rampant on reserves; government agents were hostile; and the young men, even his adopted son, Poundmaker, were ready for all-out war. But in May 1883, the aging Crowfoot intervened to allow the CPR to push through Blackfoot lands, and in 1885, five years before his death, he averted a bloodbath when he refused to join with the Métis and Cree in the North-West Rebellion.

WORKIN' ON THE RAILWAY

Impassable mountains, swamps, river valleys, endless prairies.... The 30,000 labourers who laid the miles of track for the CPR knew them all. Theirs was a life unknown to most people in this century – rough, hazardous, back-breaking and rowdy. For five years they sweated and froze, lived in tent cities, multi-decked boarding cars and false front towns. The food they ate was basic fare, and there was no booze allowed (even though anyone wanting a noggin could certainly find one if he had the money). The story of the CPR cannot be told in one or a hundred pictures, but these represent some of the days in the lives of the men who built it.

Millions of tons of rock are blasted north of Superior at Judge's Cut.

The work begins in the '70s with general surveys. This one is in B.C.

A gang of labourers crowds the paymaster's car (centre) at Rogers Pass.

The bridge over Nepigon River. It takes two years to complete the span.

The first crew is laying down ties; behind them, a flatcar with rails.

Andrew Onderdonk's forge at Yale, B.C., with a blacksmith and sons (rear).

West of Rogers Pass, Illecillewaet's finest musicians quaff a pint of ale.

The key to carrying rails and tools along the treacherous Fraser River was Onderdonk's paddle steamer Skuzzy. *Chinese workers guided the boat through the rapids by mooring lines.*

quarries along the route of the work; and he erected three explosives factories in the heart of the most forbidding Canadian wilderness. The rail workers developed the technique of blasting a path for the track through the rocky hills, then dumping the rock in nearby bogs as fill to support the oncoming line. It was lethal work. One treacherous stretch of muskeg sucked in the track seven consecutive times, swallowing up three locomotives for good measure. Sandford Fleming reported on a trip through the region in the summer of 1883, "Rude graves on the hillside mark the violent death of the poor workmen who suffered from the careless handling of that dangerous explosive, nitro-glycerine."

"Operation Skuzzy"

Andrew Onderdonk encountered the same brutal problems, and a few special ones, in his epic railroad-building through the mountains of British Columbia. A talented young engineer from New York City (he later built the tunnel under New York's East River), Onderdonk, with backing from a Wall Street financier group, won contracts from the government to construct most of the line in British Columbia. In the same flamboyant style as Van Horne, he took great gambles, defying the impossibilities of his task. When the supply of North American and British navvies dried up, he imported cheap labour from China; he revitalized the decaying Cariboo Trail, built during the 1860s gold rush days, to transport railroad equipment to the interior; and he launched the paddlewheeler *Skuzzy* on the turbulent upper Fraser River.

"Operation *Skuzzy*" began in the spring of 1882 when Onderdonk saw that, if he had a supply boat carrying tools and rails along the Fraser from Boston Bar to Lytton, he could speed up construction. But to reach Boston Bar, *Skuzzy* had to negotiate sixteen miles of rough Fraser River water, through Hell's Gate, through "gorges whose rock walls turned daylight into dusk, whose sheer volume of water threatened to sweep any ship downstream."

Two experienced white water skippers attempted the run and failed. Only Onderdonk still believed the ship could reach Boston Bar; and on September 7, *Skuzzy* launched her third brave attempt. For ten despairing days, she crashed into the Fraser's rapids without making any headway. Then Onderdonk ordered ring bolts drilled into the rock walls of the canyons and ropes strung through them from the ship; he stationed 125 Chinese workers along the canyon's rim and he told them to pull on the ropes for all they were worth. With the Chinese tugging, the paddlewheel churning, the ship's timbers groaning, *Skuzzy* inched through Hell's Gate. It was hand-over-hand work and it took six more days of aching effort, but on September 23 *Skuzzy* sailed grandly into the harbour at Boston Bar. Onderdonk put her immediately to work.

tough, dogged characters

The "Onderdonk line," as this section of the CPR came to be known on the coast, covered little more than 400 miles. But the route through nearly impassable mountain country required Herculean efforts. Onderdonk's men blasted millions of tons of rock and hollowed out fifteen tunnels, one of them 1,600 feet long. In a particular five-mile stretch near Lytton, Onderdonk explained in a report to Van Horne, his men were called on to shift 200,000 cubic yards of solid rock, 90,000 of loose rock and 400,000 of plain earth, not counting, of course, the additional tons of earth and rock they moved to drill a 400-foot tunnel. "The five miles," Onderdonk concluded in typical matter-of-fact understatement, "is as heavy as any miles in British Columbia."

The men who performed the prodigies of work for Onderdonk and for the other engineers across the prairies were as remarkable as their bosses. Tough, dogged characters, they left their own permanent mark on the West. "No class of men are so peculiar," wrote Sandford Fleming. "They are not perfect in many respects. Some are sensual, brutal and self-indulgent. But they are not all of this character. If the mass of them have any trait which is at all in prominence, it is their respect for straightforward dealing and regard for what is natural."

life in the work camps

The men learned their "straightforward dealing" the hard way – by living in cramped, close quarters with their fellow workers. During the swift track-laying across the prairies, they were quartered in special two-storey railway cars – on top, the sleeping quarters for eighty men per car and below, the mess. The cars frequently turned into fetid, claustrophobic dungeons and, when straightforward dealing gave way to bad tempers, the Mounties moved in to break up the brawls. "I cannot permit the occasion to pass," Van Horne wrote to Commissioner Irvine of the N.W.M.P. on January 1, 1883, "without acknowledging the obligations of the Company to the North-West Mounted Police whose zeal and industry in preserving order along the line under construction have contributed so much to the successful prosecution of the work."

Life became slightly less tense for the rail workers when the line reached into the Rockies and they established themselves in more permanent camps. The most sophisticated of all the work camps sprang out of the mountains near Kicking Horse Pass at a spot dubbed Holt City after the proprietor of the local railroad general store, Tim Holt. Among other amenities, Holt City boasted a

**William Cornelius Van Horne
The Boss of the CPR**

He was born and raised in poverty in Chelsea, Illinois. In 1857, at age fourteen he left school to become a telegraph operator on the Illinois Central and through years of hard work, curiosity and determination earned a reputation as one of the most capable railway men in the U.S. In 1881, James J. Hill convinced him to join the CPR and move along lagging construction. He kept track of dollars and cents, refused to accept second-best from his employees and suppliers, and personally oversaw the smallest details of the project. Van Horne was a man of incredible energy, a tireless worker, but one who always found time for his other passions: geology, art, exercise, food, wine, chess and poker. When the last spike of the CPR was driven in November 1885, he had achieved what all others thought impossible. President of the CPR from 1888-99, chairman till 1910, he died in 1915.

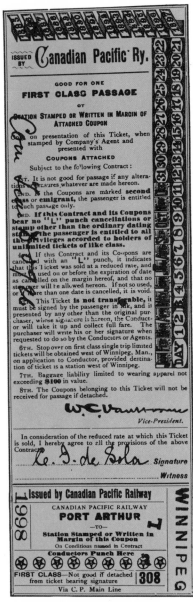

The first first-class ticket on the first transcontinental CPR train was sold to Clarence I. de Sola, a Jewish commercial traveller from Montreal, a man who in later years distinguished himself in the cause of civil rights for Jews in Canada.

collection of dormitory tents for the men, a large shed that served as a railway station, another office shed for the draughtsmen and engineers, a parked railroad car to accommodate the chief of construction, James Ross, and his wife, and a scattering of Brobdingnagian-sized tents that functioned variously as hotels, stores and a billiard parlour. Most of the social life revolved around the post office tent. It peddled cigars as well as stamps and offered a couple of beds covered with buffalo skins, a table stacked with month-old newspapers, two benches and a huge pot-bellied stove to ward off the mountain chill.

Sometimes the living seemed almost comfortable at Holt City. Certainly the food was plentiful and substantial. It was liquor that created the critical problems. To restrain the bootlegging and drunkenness that plagued construction across the prairies, the federal government passed the Act for the Preservation of Peace on Public Works, forbidding the sale of liquor within a ten-mile radius of the railway right of way. But the Act grew increasingly difficult for the Mounties to enforce, particularly when British Columbia, anxious for new sources of revenues, issued liquor-vending licences to any applicant in the railroad camps.

wild west towns

American bootleggers, gamblers, prostitutes and thieves moved their operations north to prey on the CPR navvies in the new tent and shack towns. Silver City, Beaver Creek, Golden City, even once peaceful Holt City, rechristened Laggan (now Lake Louise), ballooned into wild west towns. Robbers worked the roads by night and Mounties took to escorting every CPR paymaster.

The troubles came to a turbulent boil in the spring of 1885. Most of the navvies were broke, fleeced by the gamblers and girls, and, to make matters worse, they were short by several weeks'

pay. The CPR head office, in financial difficulties, had stalled payment to the railroad contractors who, in turn, delayed paying their workers' salaries. On the morning of April 1, three hundred of the men talked themselves into a fury. Fortified by a local bootlegger, they set out down the tracks to demand payment at the offices in Beaver Creek. Along the route they picked up more strikers and intimidated the non-strikers.

the last bad moment

Turner Bone was astounded to see the mob bearing down on his work site at the bridge near Mountain Creek. "The strikers were massed on the ground below; and they called on the carpenters to stop work and come down off the bridge. But the carpenters were in no way minded to join the strike. I saw one striker take an axe and cut the rope in the block-and-tackle arrangement by which the material was being hoisted. Down dropped the load with a crash . . . . There was nothing more to be said, so [we] yielded and called the carpenters off the bridge."

By the time the strikers reached Beaver Creek, they numbered nearly five hundred men, loaded with bravado, armed with a few pistols and cheered on by the town's resident outlaws and drunks. Inspector Sam Steele, who commanded a detachment of eight Mounties in Beaver Creek, was laid low with mountain fever that day, and he dispatched Sergeant Fury and three constables to pacify the strikers. Some of the mob began to manhandle Fury and, at that impertinence, Steele shook off his bed clothes, grabbed his Winchester, strode to the front of the advancing crowd and ordered the Justice of the Peace to read the Riot Act. "If I find more than twelve of you standing together or any large crowd assembled," Steele shouted when the J.P. had finished his reading, "I will open fire and mow you down!"

It was an authentic wild west showdown – and the mob instantly gave in. The Mounties put the leaders under arrest and, for good measure, took along a lady of the town who had taken the opportunity of the disturbance to call Steele, to his face, "a red-coated son of a bitch." The strike was over, but, largely because of the commotion they had created, the workers all received their back pay by April 7.

It was the railroad's last bad moment. Track-laying picked up tempo through the mountains in the late spring of 1885, and the difficult work north of Lake Superior neared completion. Van Horne convinced the country that the CPR was indispensable when, in a miraculous seven days, troops arrived from the East by rail to meet the challenge of Louis Riel and his Métis and Indian brethren.

On May 18, 1885, an engineer drove a ceremonial spike into a rail at Jackfish Bay on Lake Superior to complete the track in a continuous line from Montreal to the Rockies. Donald Smith, a CPR director, drove another last spike at Craigellachie in the British Columbia mountains on November 7, 1885, marking the finished route from the East to Port Moody near the coast. When Smith was done, the rail workers had their fun driving scores of extra "last spikes." Van Horne was there at Craigellachie, but he didn't bother with the spike-driving. "All I have to say," he announced, "is that the work was well done in every way."

Vancouver gave in to the same madness on May 23, 1887, when the first transcontinental passenger train pulled into *its* station. There was no further to go. The railroad was complete. Trains, linking the country, now left Montreal for Vancouver six days a week, carrying tourists, settlers, equipment, and supplies for the New West. They made the journey in a mere 86 hours, according to the CPR information guide. Van Horne insisted it was 85 hours. He may have been right. He usually was.

VAN HORNE

THOMAS HARKNESS & SONS LIMITED

No one knows whether it was in recognition of his railway building or his insatiable appetite for the choicest cigars, but Thomas Harkness & Sons, Cigar Merchants of Montreal, boxed a line of their finest (and longest) imports under the Van Horne label.

THE GOLDEN NORTH~WEST

It was the country's biggest advertising campaign, selling the "Golden Northwest" to farmers and potential emigrants in the East and abroad. After all, what good was a trans-continental railway if all it did was connect a city on the west coast with Winnipeg and the commercial capitals of the East? As soon as the railhead reached the Rockies, the promotion began. Posters, pamphlets, space ads in newspapers and magazines and touring exhibits appeared. The mastermind of the campaign in England was Alexander Begg, a public relations expert without peer who used every possible slogan and advertising vehicle to sell the image of Canada as a home for all people. Behind the campaign, of course, was the CPR itself. With its financial future in the balance, and creditors and shareholders looking for a return on investments, the first thing on president George Stephen's mind was to populate the prairies and make the railway dream begin to pay for itself.

Under the direction of L. Armstrong (seated, above left), the CPR advertising car toured eastern Ontario and Quebec. On display (left) were 4-lb. potatoes, 150-lb. squash, and 15-ft. grain. Amazed farmers were reminded, however, not to squeeze the merchandise.

This poster is from the travelling show of 1884 directed at eastern Ontario.

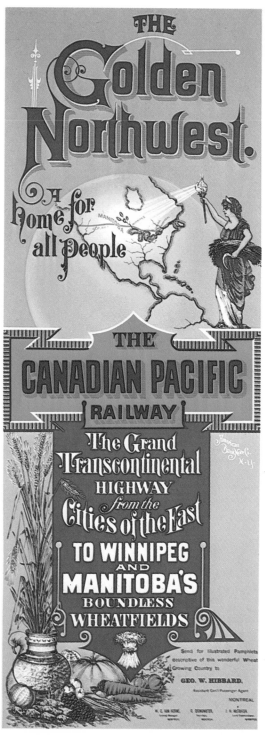

Stunning in colour, design and printing, posters painted the Utopia of the West.

It was a "Red Letter Day" when the first through-train left Montreal on June 28.

Highlight of Montreal's Winter Carnival was the Ice Palace in Dominion Square. In 1889, 25,000 blocks were cut to build the 164 foot by 155 foot structure.

CHAPTER TWO

THE MARK OF GOOD BREEDING

Why not call in the world to see us . . . in the gaiety and fervour of our mid-winter sports?

Robert McGibbon, Montreal, 1882

Robert McGibbon was the most go-ahead young man in Montreal. At the tender age of twenty-four, he had established himself as the man to watch in a downtown Montreal law firm. He had joined the Canadian Club for its good lunch-hour talk and the Atheneum Club for its good after-dinner talk (Mark Twain addressed both groups in 1881); he attended concerts of the brand new Montreal Philharmonic, which boasted a choir of 250 voices; and he drank at that favourite rendezvous for Montreal lawyers and judges, the bar of St. Lawrence Hall, Henry Hogan's fading but elegant old hotel. But McGibbon reserved his real enthusiasm for the Snowshoe Club because, most of all, he loved the Montreal winter.

The Snowshoe Club had blossomed from its modest beginnings in 1840 into a splendidly active organization of over four hundred members. It staged evening hikes from the McGill University gates up Peel Street or Côte des Neiges to the "Pines" on Mount Royal. It organized races (including a 120-yard hurdles contest on snowshoes) at the Lacrosse Grounds on Sherbrooke Street. On weekends it planned cross-country runs to towns ten or twelve miles away, with

evenings of biscuits, cheese, beer and song afterwards. And once a season, it dispatched a dozen of the hardiest members on a four-day, forty-five mile tramp to the town of St. Andrews. The club's annual meetings, needless to say, had serious matters to deal with, and nothing was more serious than the proposal offered by young McGibbon towards the end of the 1882 meeting.

"Why not call in the world," McGibbon demanded, "to see us as we are in the gaiety and fervour of our mid-winter sports?" The meeting caught fire at the idea of a winter carnival. George Iles, the publicity-conscious manager of the Windsor Hotel, promised the services of his hostelry, the finest in Canada. A Grand Trunk Railway member pledged his company's financial support. Other businessmen followed suit, and the meeting adjourned in a ring of enthusiasm after appointing as chairman of the first annual Montreal Winter Carnival – Robert McGibbon.

The following year, thousands of visitors, attracted by the carnival committee's enthusiastic campaign, enjoyed Montreal's four-day extravaganza: skating races; hockey matches; lacrosse games played on ice; snowshoe races over a steeplechase course laid out on the McGill University grounds; curling bonspiels held at night under the glare of twenty electric lights strung over the frozen St. Lawrence at the foot of McGill Street; and parades of ornately decorated sleighs swishing

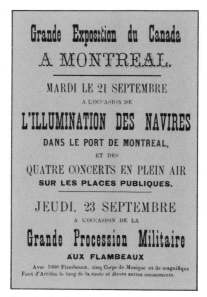

No city in the country could match Montreal's spectacular celebrations. In September 1882, organizers strung electric lights across the river at the foot of McGill Street to light the harbour for seasonal festivities.

25

Donald A. Smith
The Power-Broker

Donald Smith was born in Scotland in 1820, the son of a tradesman. In 1838 he joined the Hudson's Bay Co. as an apprentice clerk, and in thirty years worked his way to become chief commissioner in Canada, the HBC's major shareholder by '83 and governor by 1889. Having entered politics as an MLA for Manitoba, then MP for Selkirk, his withdrawal of support for John A. Macdonald, embroiled in the Pacific Scandal of 1873, helped cause the Tory government to resign. Subsequently obliged to remain a silent member of the CPR syndicate, Smith and his cousin George Stephen were the financial brains that kept the railway afloat during many crises, and a reconciliation with John A. coincided with the honour of driving the ceremonial last spike of the CPR.

up Sherbrooke Street behind pairs of high-stepping thoroughbreds. On downtown streets closed off for the carnival, revellers plunged down toboggan slides, one a breathtaking 2,400 feet long. And there was the magnificent fancy-dress skating ball at Victoria Rink. "Half Montreal died of envy," one newspaper reported, "while the other half crammed the rink galleries and sat ten deep in spaces hardly enough for five."

roman candles and rockets

But the main event was the mock epic attack on the Ice Palace in Dominion Square on opening night. The Palace itself was of heroic proportions. Constructed from blocks of ice forty inches long by twenty wide and fifteen thick, it stood ninety feet square with thirty-foot towers at each corner and a central column soaring eighty feet into the air; it bore all the military frills of battlements, loopholes in the walls and interior winding staircases. Behind the battlements and loopholes on the night of the attack clustered several dozen members of the carnival committee supported by an even hundred soldiers from the Victoria Rifles, all equipped for battle with roman candles and skyrockets.

Just before eight o'clock, the attacking army surged into view, marching resolutely down Peel Street. These foot soldiers, one thousand strong, all wearing snowshoes and decked out in moccasins, tuques with long tassels and thick white blanket coats, were also armed with roman candles and rockets. And in one shattering moment the night burst into a noon-hour brilliance. Both armies opened fire with their rockets. Electric lights flashed on over the square. Torches winked from all sides. The roar was tumultuous. The sounds of battle quivered the eardrum. Off in the rear, the Victoria Rifles Band struck up a martial air. But no one, except the band members, could hear the tune. The audience – a happy, stomping, cheering

MONTREAL MANSIONS

The *Illustrated Atlas of the Dominion of Canada* (1881) captured the architectural opulence of Montreal: "Its numerous beautiful villas, orchards, and delightful drives, its grand and stately edifices... present to the view a grand panorama."

An afternoon with Mr. & Mrs. Sergeant at "Weredale" in 1885. Note the four busy domestics in background.

Mrs. George Stephen's drawing room. The portrait is of her husband, president of the CPR and Bank of Montreal.

Donald Smith's cut-stone mansion c. 1880 at the corner of Dorchester and Fort Streets, demolished in 1941.

crowd – numbered 25,000 or 60,000 depending on which newspaper account you read next day. The papers did agree on two facts – the attacking Snowshoe brigade triumphed in the battle and Robert McGibbon's first Montreal Winter Carnival was a smashing success.

Only Montreal, of all Canadian cities in the 1880s, would presume to pull off anything quite so dramatic, ridiculous and grand as a staged assault on a palace made of ice. Montreal was the one true metropolitan centre that Canada could boast (its population in 1881 was 140,747, compared to Toronto's 86,415). And, like metropolises in any country at any time, it displayed itself in expensive games, lavish behaviour and eccentric characters. Montreal shook and wavered and bustled with every sort of fun and action and tragedy; it was altogether a rowdy, slick, busy, beguiling place.

baronial castles

Every extreme existed, especially violent contrasts in wealth and poverty. Donald Smith built a home in the eighties at 1157 Dorchester Street that resembled a baronial castle. It had an art gallery, a ballroom large enough to accommodate an orchestra and several hundred waltzing couples, one porcelain bath and one marble bath, custom-made furniture carved from bird's eye maple, and a three-storey staircase so elaborate in its carpentry and cabinet work that it alone cost $50,000 to install. In 1889, the same year that Donald Smith was moving into his castle, workers at the Macdonald Tobacco Plant in Montreal were telling the Royal Commission on Labor and Capital that their average wage for a sixty-hour week ranged from $6.00 to $8.50. One father testified that his fourteen-year-old son earned $1.60 per week at another tobacco plant but that the boy had been fined $1.75 for insolence in his first week. The company was demanding its fifteen cents.

This menu of the private farewell dinner given in honour of Mr. George Goldie "on the eve of his departure from Montreal to British Columbia" on May 15, 1888, is a fine example of graphic design and gourmet delights.

Shoppers and loiterers line Notre Dame St. in Montreal's business district. Horse-drawn wagons rattle across street railway tracks. Gardner's Tavern and Restaurant (left) is the place to go for lunch.

Ghettos formed easily in Montreal. The Irish kept to their preserve in the southwest corner of the city, in a section called Griffintown named after Robert Griffin, who leased the area in 1820 from the Grey Nuns for 99 years. Griffintown's people were mainly Catholics from Southern Ireland. Unlike the more well-to-do immigrants from Protestant Ulster who settled in Ontario, they couldn't afford to travel any farther in Canada than the port where they'd landed. In Griffintown they recreated a slice of Ireland, complete with their own shops, schools, churches and prejudices.

few common characteristics

St. Lawrence Main Street, which ran straight up from the St. Lawrence, defined an even more significant social and racial split within the city. To the east lived French-speaking Montrealers and to the west, English-speaking Montrealers. In each area, commerce and industry clustered close to the harbour, and the residential areas sloped back from the water and up the mountain, the homes growing more splendid as they spread northward. But apart from the similarity in town planning, the areas shared few common characteristics.

East Montreal was largely working class, supplying the manpower for the city's thriving industries in tobacco and textiles and for the grand new CPR shops. In personality, it displayed all the modest ease of a rural Quebec village. Few people spoke English there. Life was simple and thrifty. It revolved around *maman*, who dominated the family, and a handful of organizations that ordered life outside the family: the St. Vincent de Paul Association looked after the poor; the Union St. Joseph tended to the workers' needs; the Church regulated things of the spirit; and when a man wanted to save or borrow, he approached a benevolent guild. In the mid-eighties only one commercial bank, was operating in East Montreal.

West Montreal's atmosphere was aggressively cosmopolitan. "Sherbrooke Street", enthused the authors of *Picturesque Montreal*, "is scarcely surpassed by the Fifth Avenue of New York in the magnificence of its buildings. The grounds include demesne and parks, the charm of the country and the rush and roar of a great commercial centre." The sweep of change and contrast was every bit as vivid as *Picturesque Montreal* suggests. The city had installed an electric street-lighting system by the end of 1882; but on the meandering streets near the waterfront, the electricity illuminated some of the oldest buildings in North America, elegant reminders of the French regime – the Château de Ramezay, dating from 1705, and the gracefully aged Bécancour family house on Jacques Cartier Square. Corporations were erecting mighty new office buildings in the business district, modernistic limestone fortresses like the Temple and the New York Life Building on St. James and the CPR headquarters on Windsor. But a few blocks to the east, the hustle and bustle around Bonsecours Market every Tuesday and Friday seemed ancient and timeless, with the lines of creaking country carts and the stalls of fruits and vegetables spilling along the streets and squares.

taking religion seriously

The heart of Montreal offered an equal number of churches and saloons. "This is the first time I ever was in a city where you couldn't throw a brick without breaking a church window," Mark Twain told guests at a dinner in his honour at the Windsor Hotel in 1881. There were sixty churches in the city that year. The Cathedral of St. James, just going up at the corner of Dorchester Street and Dominion Square, resembled a small-scale version of St. Peter's in Rome. St. Andrew's Church sat on Beaver Hall Hill looking like Salisbury Cathedral in miniature. The Parish Church of Notre Dame, with its 10,000 seats, was the second largest cathedral in North America and boasted the eighth largest bell in the world, its fifteen-ton *Le Gros Bourdon*. Montreal took religion seriously. When St. Paul's Presbyterian Church needed a new preacher in 1883, it promptly imported the Reverend Dr. James Barclay of Edinburgh at the annual stipend of $750.

a flamboyant Irishman

As a local celebrity, Dr. Barclay could not rival the fame of Joe Beef, king of Montreal's tavern proprietors. Saloons and cafés lined the waterfront in the same density that churches dotted the streets north of it. They were mostly foul, dank places where beer cost five cents for a pint-and-a-half mug and where the clientèle included, as one contemporary account put it, "the homeless and footloose of the world." But Joe Beef's Canteen, operated by a flamboyant Irishman whose real name was Charles McKiernan, was unique. Joe Beef's generosity to his regular patrons seemed unlimited. When workers on the Lachine Canal went on strike in July 1878, demanding a raise from eighty cents to a dollar for a ten-hour day, Beef distributed among their families three thousand loaves of bread and five hundred gallons of soup. Then at his own expense he sent two delegations of men to argue their case in Ottawa. At his wife's funeral, the bereaved Beef ordered a band to play the "Dead March" from *Saul* on the way to Mount Royal Cemetery and to swing into "The Girl I Left Behind" on the return trip. For Beef's own funeral, in 1889, offices were closed, labourers given a half-holiday, and the line of mourners stretched for blocks.

Life uptown, in the residential districts, was more sedate. The wealthiest section, home territory for the Scots who dominated Montreal business

Louis Fréchette
The Voice of an Exile

Like many restless young men of his time, Louis-Honoré Fréchette was a radical, an idealist and a romantic. Born in Lévis, Quebec, in 1839, he attended Laval University and set up a law practice in 1864. A vocal supporter of the Liberal *Rouges*, he aroused the wrath of the Church and the establishment, and in 1865 moved to Chicago. While in the U.S. he published *La Voix d'un exilé* in 1868, a strong anti-Confederation, pro-annexation collection of poems. He returned to Quebec in 1871, and was elected to parliament for a term. After *Les Fleurs boréales* (1879) won the French Academy's Prix Montyon, he came to be regarded as the most provocative and important voice in what his mentor, Octave Crémazie, called the wilderness of Québecois writing. *La Légende d'un peuple* (1887) is his most polished volume, a celebration of the historical events and people of French Canadian history.

Joe Beef of Montreal, the Son of the People.

He cares not for Pope, Priest, Parson or King William of the Boyne; all Joe wants is the Coin. He trusts in God in summer time to keep him from all harm; when he sees the frost and snow poor ol l Joe trusts to the Almighty Dollar and good old maple wood to keep his belly warm, for Churches, Chapels, Ranters, Preachers, Beechers and such stuff Montreal has already got enough.

FROM THE 'EVENING STAR," APRIL 15, 1876.

Mr. John Dougall in the New York *Witness*, makes an appeal for " additional capital to the extent of fifty thousand dollars." He proposes to issue bonds of $10, $50, $100 and $500, payable in five years, and bearing 7 per cent. interest.

JOE BEEF.

Any citizens, this day, having any of their Bonds on Hand, will please call at my Office from 10 a.m. to 12 a.m. daily, or at next door, the Rag Store, and they will get their full value, as far as old paper goes.

All you Clergymen, Captains, Sailors, Bums, and Scurvy-Tailors, if you can walk or crawl, when you go on the spree, go and see JOE BEEF of Montreal.

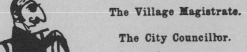

The Village Magistrate.

The City Councillor.

The Sunday School Bouncer.

The Blooming Rose with the Temperance Nose.

All you Clergymen, Captains, Sailors, Bums and Scurvy-Tailors, if you can walk or crawl, when you go on the spree, go and see JOE BEEF of Montreal.

Probably the most colourful bar in the city of Montreal was Joe Beef's. The man who "cared not for Pope, Priest or King William of the Boyne" had a knack for advertising that attracted Montreal's workers by the droves to his door.

The message on this 1882 greeting card is a gag, of course–one of the unusual bits of humorous nostalgia that has survived from the days of our hard-drinking grandfathers.

and finance, lay between Beaver Hall Hill and the foot of Mount Royal and between Dorchester and Sherbrooke Streets. The new houses along Sherbrooke, reflecting the life-style of their owners, were substantial, comfortable and solemn.

Senator George Drummond's showplace mansion at the corner of Sherbrooke and Metcalfe sported a tower, two gables rising steeply to grotesque beasts, an ornamented sandstone porch, an oriel window and balcony and a general sprinkling of carvings and ornaments, all of these designed to create an impression of solid grandeur.

The rich of Montreal were masters of the grand gesture. Peter Redpath, the reserved west Montreal millionaire reached for the grand effect one night in 1880 when he rose at a banquet marking old Dr. Dawson's twenty-fifth anniversary as president of McGill and announced with orotund precision that he, Peter Redpath, would personally see to the building of the university's very own museum. He was of course as good as his word – the Redpath Museum, costing $100,000. opened in 1882. In 1887, with the same sense of grandeur, Donald Smith and George Stephen

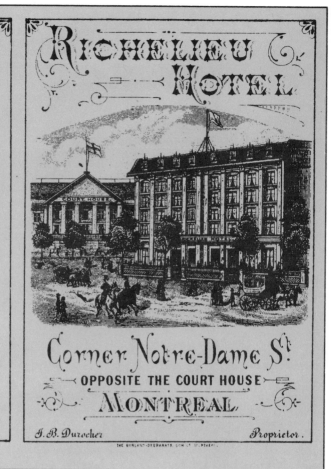

Louis Cyr
Heavyweight Champ of the World

He was the kind of guy you didn't want to cross–a legend in his own time and still a legend almost a hundred years later. Louis Cyr was born in St. Cyprian, Lower Canada, in 1863. One of *seventeen* children, he left school at age twelve to work as a lumberjack. Legend has it that at seventeen he carried a loaded farm wagon out of the mud on his back. Like many other Québecois, he sought work in the U.S. during the hard times of the late seventies, but he returned to Montreal in 1882 as a policeman. He was 6'1" in height, 267 lbs., a large man by the day's standards, and one who knew show-biz in the era of spectacles. In 1885 he won the weight-lifting-championship of North America, seven years later the world championship in London, and throughout the '90s he dazzled the crowds for P.T. Barnum's circus.

Unlike Joe Beef's (opposite), the Richelieu Hotel was one of the fashionable establishments of Montreal in the eighties. A room on the American plan (meals included) cost $2.00-2.50 per day for M. Durocher's finest comforts.

donated one million dollars for a new hospital – the Royal Victoria, completed in 1893.

In all of Montreal's houses, great and humble, home-entertaining was the vogue of the eighties. Tea parties, oyster parties, magic-lantern-picture parties and kettle drum parties – everyone threw them and everyone came to them. The hosts served sandwiches, pound cake, tea, coffee and lemonade (liquor rarely appeared on the side tables), and the guests discussed the marvels of the day, ranging from phrenology to Montreal's Strongest Man In The World, Louis Cyr.

Dinner parties were either marathon ordeals or a glutton's delight, depending on the guest's appetite. Hostesses believed in setting a groaning board. Apart from the elaborate decorations – a silver-plated epergne, crystal candy baskets and fluted flower vases were customary – the table was filled with tureens of soup, platters of fish and oysters, and a variety of game or creamed dishes. That was merely the first course. It was followed in relentless procession by roasts, fish, pies, seasonal vegetables, rice croquettes, hominy, sauces and jellies, custards and pies, fruits and nuts and

Province of Quebec
Rifle Association.

COTE ST. LUC RANGES.

Wednesday Afternoon, August 14th,

1889.

PROGRAMME.
(BAND OF THE VICTORIA RIFLES.)

1. March, - "Our Colonel," - Krein.
2. Waltz, - "Dernier Sourire," - Klein.
3. Overture, "Jeanne Maillotte" - Reynaud.
4. Piccolo Solo, - "Caprice," - Douard.
   SIGNOR CAMILLO MAGGIO.
5. The British Patrol, - - Asch.
6. Polka, - "Pschutt," - Mayeur.
7. Waltz, - "Souvenir de Cluses," - Estace.
8. Selection, - "Erminie," - Jacobovoski.
9. March, - "Victoria Rifles," - Hardy.
10. Galop, - "Sportsman," - Wiegand.

MR. EDMOND HARDY, BAND MASTER.

One of the most popular sports of the age was shooting, and Quebec's Rifle Association was the focus of Canadian marksmanship in the '80s. This programme of band music for a Wednesday afternoon meet includes one composition by the leader of the Victoria Rifles' Band, Mr. Hardy.

Opposite page: The beginning of the Amateur Athletic Association of Canada occurred in 1884, when the Montreal association, whose medals are pictured here, invited groups from Hamilton, Toronto, Kingston, Brantford and Ottawa to join in the first national sports federation.

coffee. Each course was accompanied by wine – Chablis with small oysters, sherry after soup, champagne with roasts and burgundy with game.

Theatrical parties were all the rage. Charades and blind-man's-buff rivalled tableaux evenings, when groups of guests enacted literary scenes in two-minute tableau arrangements while someone read the relevant passage – Tennyson's *Maude* and Longfellow's *Evangeline* were favourites. The theatrical games were an acceptable way of blowing off a little steam in a time when a Canadian version of Victorianism inhibited many social relations. "Suppression of undue emotion," instructed *Our Deportment* "whether of laughter, of anger, of mortification, of disappointment, or of selfishness in any form, is a mark of good breeding."

the vaccination riot

In the roaringly active Montreal outdoor life of the eighties, the toboggan girl, with her jersey sash, ankle-length skirt and long-laced moccasins, was the "sweater girl" of her day. The seventies had seen the development of formal organizations of all Montreal's sporting activities, and by 1885 there were also a cricket club, a baseball club, three football clubs and a cycling organization with seventy members. The golf course, begun in 1873 at Lord Dufferin's urging, was going strong, and many young men were beginning to take up tennis rackets. But lacrosse was king. Of the nine lacrosse teams in the city, the most active were the Shamrocks, with their grounds on St. Catherine Street, and the Montreal Club, with their field on Sherbrooke. Games between these two teams made lacrosse into a spectator sport that attracted thousands to a playing field.

With all the prosperity and progress, an essential spirit at times deserted Montreal. One February day in 1885, a Pullman porter from a train on the Chicago run showed up at the Hôtel Dieu Hospital complaining of a skin eruption. The hospital's doctors diagnosed the affliction as smallpox. By the end of that year at least three thousand citizens had died of smallpox, and probably many more victims of the disease were quietly buried by relatives too frightened or too ashamed to report the true cause of death. The epidemic had reached a peak in the summer months and, at the urging of Dr. William Hingston of Hôtel Dieu, the city ordered compulsory vaccinations. Be vaccinated – or go to jail. It was a necessary, if belated, civic measure, but superstition in the poorer quarters of the city caused a resistance. When the vaccinating teams tried to enter homes, they were hurled into the street.

In September a mob rioted in protest against the vaccination programme. They set off for City Hall from the east end, hurling stones through drug store windows and setting fires as they moved. One blaze on St. Catherine Street raged out of control, and when the fire brigade and the police arrived to combat the flames, they had to fight off the mob first. The police chief was an early casualty and, convinced that the struggle was beyond his men, summoned the Victoria Rifles. The army, 1,340 strong, finally silenced the mob, threw the leaders into jail and sent their followers tumbling back to the east end. For the rest of the year, until the epidemic had run its cruel course, the doctors travelled with armed escorts.

a bitter legacy

But it wasn't an epidemic that left the most bitter and durable legacy of the eighties to Montreal. It was the hanging of Louis Riel on November 16, 1885, two thousand miles to the west. And even though Montreal remained the city of the grand gesture, the division between French and English Montrealers, deepened by this crisis, marked the last years of the decade.

STUDENTS OF ART & LIFE

During the years when romantic landscapes dominated the realm of Canadian painting, a coterie of young Canadian artists was living in the Bohemian Left-Bank sector of Paris, studying art under the academic French masters of the day. Discipline at the private academies and the Ecole des Beaux-Arts was strict, emphasizing detail and precision in portraiture and figure painting. The neo-classical routine at the Académie Julian so annoyed twenty-three-year-old William Brymner of Ottawa that he wrote to his father: "Corpses, corpses, corpses . . . how the French love them!"

But Paris left its mark on the work of these artists. The group, Brymner, George Reid of Wingham, Ont., Paul Peel of London, Ont., Robert Harris of Charlottetown, P.E.I., and Ozias Leduc of St. Hilaire, Que., returned to Canada with a style of painting that influenced the just-born Royal Canadian Academy and the art schools and societies.

Paul Peel's stunning figure studies of the eighties, like Venetian Bather, *scandalized the Canadian art world until his work won the French Salon's medal. The French actress Sarah Bernhardt tried to buy one of his paintings but couldn't afford it. Before he could show his full genius, Peel died at thirty-one.*

While George Reid's Forbidden Fruit *(1889) is a fine example of the French influence, his work is unique in its use of Canadian subjects, themes and settings.*

Robert Harris, commissioned in 1882 to paint The Fathers of Confederation, *had his training in Boston, London and Paris.* Harmony, *a study of his sister-in-law playing the organ, is one of the best examples of Harris' treatment of themes and forms.*

Left: *William Brymner's* A Wreath of Flowers *(1884) won him critical acclaim in London and election to the newly formed Royal Canadian Academy of Arts.*

As the railway stretched across the country, creating towns throughout the prairies, journalists from the east, like T.B. Braden and A.M. Armour, arrived in the vanguard of settlers to establish newspapers and journals to cover the excitement. On August 10, 1883, a day before the railhead reached Calgary, Braden arrived in town, struck up a partnership with Armour, set up offices in a tent (see page 41) and three weeks later published the first edition of the Herald. *Two years later, on the day Big Bear's surrender signalled the end of the North-West rebellion, the front page of the* Herald *was crowded with gossipy announcements and news–everything from the loss of one corduroy coat in Calgary to the ill-treatment of Catholic prisoners in Toronto jails. Nothing on the page seems to reflect the paper's editorial policy to remedy any "manifest abuses" that came to its attention.*

The Herald.

Vol I. CALGARY, ALBERTA, JULY 2, 1885. No. 1.

TELEGRAPHIC.

FORT PITT.

STRAUBENZIE, June 29.— It was intended to make the start for home immediately on the arrival of Gen. Strange's column, but the programme has been altered, owing to two companies of the 65th (Montreal) battalion and one company of the Winnipeg Light Infantry having been left at various places between Calgary and Edmonton. These companies are now coming down the river on scows, and on the steamer Baroness, which left this afternoon to meet them. No move will be made until the steamer returns, which will be four days from this. The start will then certainly be made.

In a shooting match to-day the Royal Grenadiers, of Toronto, beat the 9th and Midland battalions.

MEDICINE HAT.

MEDICINE HAT, July 1.—The detachments here of the 66th, Halifax battalion, received orders this morning to report at Moosejaw en route to Winnipeg. The men were overjoyed at getting the order.

WINNIPEG.

WINNIPEG, July 1.—General Manager Van Horne gave the Winnipeg civic council no satisfaction in reply to its complaint against the new change of time table in the running of trains to the boundary.

At the public meeting called yesterday, to consider the means of raising money to erect a memorial to the volunteers, but two persons attended.

OTTAWA.

OTTAWA, June 30.—Just previous to his departure for England on Friday last with the Wimbleton team, Capt. Clarke, of the 90th battalion, Winnipeg, addressed a letter to the Minister of Militia in which he praises the conduct of the men in the different engagements fought during the Northwest rebellion. Capt. Clarke was himself wounded at Fish Creek, and had some experience of the hospital corps arrangements. He eulogizes the entire surgical corps and the general treatment received at the hands of Dr. Orton, Dr. Sutherland, Dr. Roderick and others of the staff.

TORONTO.

TORONTO, July 1.—The investigation into the charges against Warden Massie, of the Central Prison, will be held on Thursday. Nicholas Murphy will represent the Catholic convention in reference to the charges preferred against Massie of ill-treating the Catholic prisoners.

HALIFAX.

HALIFAX, July 1.—The Scott Act has been carried in Gainsboro County. Only twenty Anti-Scott Act votes were polled.

NEW YORK.

NEW YORK, June 30.—Mrs. Dudley's trial, on the charge of attempting to shoot O'Donovan Rossa, has commenced. The New York Irish are exhibiting great interest in the result.

Fish, President of the Marine Bank, has been sentenced to ten years imprisonment.

LONDON.

LONDON, June 30.—Gladstone has addressed a letter to his Midlothian constituents, in which he intimates that he will again lead the Liberal party.

PARIS.

PARIS, June 30.—Rochford published this morning an Egyptian account of the death of Pain, in which the story is shown to rest on a runner whom the Mahdi subsequently killed.

Lord Salisbury is negotiating with the Porte for the occupation of Egypt by Egyptian troops to be paid by the Egyptian treasurer. This would involve an increase of twelve million pounds in the Egyptian loan. It is reported that Lord Salisbury's scheme includes the administration by England of the civil government of Egypt.

LOST.

One Corduroy Coat, with pocket book and papers, and two photos, on 3rd inst. Finder will please leave same at Herald Office.

NOTICE.

A Liberal Conservative Association has been formed in Calgary, and all Conservatives in the District are hereby invited to enroll themselves as members. It is the hope of the Association to make itself the leading one of the kind in the Territories, and the hearty co-operation of the Conservatives of the District is invited for that purpose.

STALLION.

A French-Canadian Stallion will stand for mares at Bain Bros. Livery Stable. $10 per service.
Calgary, June 23.   95-3m

WANTED.

A situation as cook for surveying, mining or ranche company. Apply to C. B. Mason, at Ambrose Shaw's, gunsmith, Atlantic avenue, opposite the depot, Calgary.

Stray Horses.

Two mares. One brown, branded B D on left shoulder; 1 chestnut, branded C on left thigh.

Have been taken up on the Little Bow. Parties are requested to prove property, pay expenses, and take away. Apply to the North-West Cattle Company.
High River, June 23   95-3in

Should this Meet the Eye

Of anyone who has met with a person of the name of George Derry (an Englishman) who took up land at Pine Creek, about 12 miles from Calgary, and who left that place in May, 1884, to go to the mountains— any information will be gladly received by his sorrowing friends who have not heard anything of him for a year. Address Mrs. George Derry, Smith's Hotel, Fort Qu'Appelle, N. W. Territory.

NOTICE.

In the matter of the Mount Royal Ranche Company (limited) in liquidation.

I am now prepared to receive offers for the purchase of the stock, plant and lease of the Mount Royal Ranche Company (limited). The lease is composed of about 12,000 acres of grazing land situated on the Ghost and Bow River, in the North-West Territories of Canada, about 35 miles from Calgary. The C. P. Railway passes across the lease. This ranche is well watered and wooded and is known as one of the best winter ranges in the North-West Territories of Canada. The improvements and plant are all first-class. There are now about one hundred and fifty horses on the range. Any further information as to same can be had on application to J. A. Gemmill, Barrister, Ottawa, John McD. Hains, Western Chambers, 22 St. John St., Montreal, or to the under signed.

HENRY BLEECKER,
Liquidator,
Mount Royal Ranche Co., Calgary, N.W.T.

NOTICE.

In the matter of the Mount Royal Ranche Company (limited) in liquidation.

I have been appointed liquidator of the above Company, now in liquidation. All persons having any claims against the said Company are notified that the same must be filed with me in fifty days from the date hereof, with dates and items and verified under oath or declaration. In case any claimant holds any security for his claim he must specify the nature and amount of such security in his claim, and must therein on his oath put a specified value thereon. After the said fifty days from the date hereof I shall proceed to distribute the assets of said Company only having notice of such claims as are properly filed with me.

HENRY BLEECKER,
Liquidator,
Mount Royal Ranche Co. (limited).
Calgary, N. W. T.,
June 24th 1885.

CHAPTER THREE

A VOICE TO EVERY CAUSE

Our aim will be to give voice to every cause and interest in the North-West . . .

Nicholas Flood Davin

In preparation for his most sensational scoop, Nicholas Flood Davin, the founder, editor, publisher and star reporter of the Regina *Leader*, decked himself out in a soutane and crucifix, a broad-brimmed hat and a fake beard, and insinuated himself into Regina's barracks prison on the night of November 15, 1885. Thus disguised as a priest on an errand of compassion, he bluffed his way into the death cell of Louis Riel, interviewed him, and then printed the human interest story of the year, perhaps of the decade.

"I bent down, told Riel I was a *Leader* reporter in the guise of a prêtre," Davin wrote, "and had come to give his last message to the world . . . 'Quick,' I said, 'have you anything to say? I have brought pencil and paper. Speak.'" Riel apparently had plenty to say. In language coloured as much by Davin's own florid prose as by Riel's high-blown oratorical style, Davin recorded for the *Leader* the last public ramblings of Louis Riel.

"'Sir John A. Macdonald! I send you a message. Do not let yourself be completely carried away by the glories of power . . . take every day a few moments . . . and prepare yourself for death.'" According to Davin's story, Riel sent

slightly wistful parting words to everyone – to his Métis comrades, to the governor general, to French Canadians, even to the general who commanded the force that defeated him. But, Davin reported, Riel was still capable of a final flourish of bravado: "'Yet the spirit tells me I should yet rule a vast country, the North-West, with power derived from heaven.'"

"I left him with some sympathy and no little sadness," Davin wrote. "I felt that I had been in the presence of a man of genius manqué, of a man who, had he been gifted with judgement, might have accomplished much."

Next day, Davin wrote another story for the *Leader*, this one written in plain documentary prose: "The body ceased to sway. It hung without a quiver. Dr. Dodd, looking at his watch and feeling the pulse of what was Riel [said:] 'He is dead. Dead in two minutes.'" But the story, displaying a measure of feeling, even admiration for Riel, a rare approach for a prairie newspaper in 1885, ended: "He died with calm courage, like a man and a Christian, and seemed to me a triumph of rationality."

Davin was a nervy, garrulous, hard-drinking Irishman who performed vivid feats in half a dozen professions in his lifetime: as an author, he published *Eos: An Epic of the Dawn*, a 141-page collection of his own poetry; as a politician, he sat as M.P. for the riding of West Assiniboia for

The first newspaper in what is now Alberta was Frank Oliver's Edmonton Bulletin. *The first edition, printed in six-point type (a little over one-sixteenth of an inch high) on a five-by-six-inch page, hit the streets in Dec. 1880 – "the world's smallest newspaper," according to Oliver.*

**John Wilson Bengough
The Man from *Grip***

J.W. Bengough, perhaps Canada's all-time best cartoonist, was certainly her liveliest political satirist, an authentic 19th-century genius. Born in Toronto in 1851, Bengough studied law briefly, but gravitated toward journalism. At twenty-two he founded the weekly humour journal *Grip*, the paper that became the scourge of the high and mighty in politics and business. Bengough was a declared advocate of the Single Tax (a radical answer to the uneven distribution of wealth), of woman suffrage and free trade, and also a vociferous fighter against alcohol, tobacco and tariffs. In 1892 he cut connections with *Grip*, by then the most successful paper of its kind, and took on jobs with the Montreal *Star* and the Toronto *Globe*. He was the author of four books, including *The Up-To-Date Primer: A book of lessons for little political economists, in words of one syllable with pictures.*

thirteen years; as a barrister, he took calls to the bars of England, Ontario and the North-West Territories – in his most celebrated case, he defended, alas unsuccessfully, the assassin of George Brown, editor of the Toronto *Globe*.

Davin had worked for the *Irish Times* in his home country and covered the Franco-German war for the London *Standard*. In 1872, the *Pall Mall Gazette* dispatched him to North America to write a series of articles on the possible annexation of Canada by the United States. Davin discovered no threat of a takeover but stayed on in Toronto. He worked as literary critic for both the *Mail* and the *Globe*, wrote a book, *The Irishman in Canada*, practised a little law, indulged his formidable appetites for good food, strong drink, witty companions and beautiful women, and enjoyed a special status as one of Sir John A.'s more roistering cronies.

the pioneer press

In the fall of 1882, when Davin was travelling across the west on a junket organized by the CPR, Regina was a city of 1,000 citizens, eight hotels, two doctors, six lawyers, three billiard parlours, and streets of impenetrable mud. But the town yearned for the prestige and recognition a newspaper would bring it, and a group of Regina citizens offered Davin $5,000 in cash and $5,000 in town lots to launch the paper for them. Davin agreed, and the following March, operating with a magnificent $20,000 press, he turned out the first issue of a brand new weekly, the Regina *Leader*.

"Our aim," Davin editorialized in that first issue, "will be to give voice to every cause and interest in the North-West which concerns the public welfare." His *Leader* championed western settlement with a series of glowing articles on the joys of prairie living, (later published in a book entitled, in his usual grandiose style, *Homes For Millions*). The paper took the lead in encouraging civic improvements; "Let us take away from Regina the reproach of being the ugliest place on the line of the CPR." And he introduced to Regina some of his own love of great literature.

Davin's dramatic flair made him more than a typical 1880s newspaperman or a typical westerner. Still, in many ways, he emerged as a representative figure of a remarkable period in western Canadian journalism. It was the age of the pioneer press, when an editor had to make up in ingenuity, style and courage what he invariably lacked in man power and equipment. In the western newspaper business of the eighties, presses were primitive and reporters hard to come by, and all the facilities that newsmen in eastern Canada accepted as a matter of course were, out west, quirkish and unreliable. "As the line has been down since Saturday between Hay Lakes and here," read the lead-off item in the very first issue of the Edmonton *Bulletin*, dated December 6, 1880, "we are without telegrams for this issue. A man will leave tomorrow to repair it, and by next week we hope to be able to give the latest news from the East up to date."

a miniature newspaper

Setting up a newspaper in the rough new prairie towns involved the back-breaking, exasperating job of carting in and installing the press equipment. Patrick Gammie Laurie, founder-editor of the Saskatchewan *Herald* of Battleford, wrote that the six-hundred-mile ox cart journey from Winnipeg to Battleford along a route that had not one bridge or ferry boat almost made him abandon his entire newspaper career. Frank Oliver of the Edmonton *Bulletin* began his operations with a miniature two-hundred-pound press because it was easier to ship from Winnipeg to Edmonton. As a result, Oliver turned out a miniature paper:

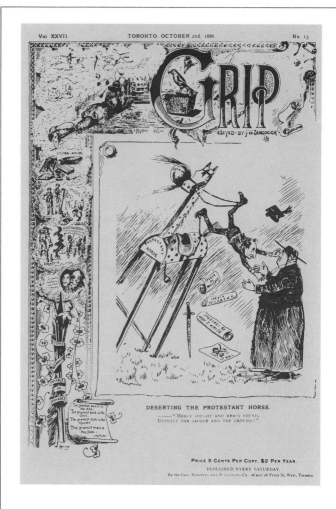

October 31, 1885: John A. stands between Justice and Mercy on the question of Riel's death sentence and the jury's recommendation.

A humdrum day in parliament, sketched from the press gallery. John A. (centre) dozes off while Blake (left) holds forth.

J.W. Bengough's *Grip*, the conscience of parliament, the prime minister, religious leaders, big businessmen, bigots, bilkers and buffoons of the '80s, was the reading treat of the week. Although self-righteous Canadians enjoyed seeing the frailties and faults of politicians caricatured in its pages, Bengough reached into every corner of society with *Grip*. Poor John A. was a perpetual target, as were most "honourable" members of parliament.(It seems Bengough had a bone to pick with almost everyone.)

Mackenzie and Brown, weeping crocodile tears, call on a rather smug John A. to implement his National Policy of protective tariffs – which had won him the '78 election during hard times.

Frank Oliver
Edmonton's Indomitable Editor

Among the curious adventurers who settled in Edmonton was a fiery young Ontario printer named Frank Oliver. Born in 1853, he had learned the trade at George Brown's *Globe* and at the *Manitoba Free Press* before packing his belongings and a printing press in 1876 and setting out on the old Carlton Trail. The trip was a near disaster – only he and his ox reached the Fort. When the telegraph line was extended to Edmonton early in 1880 and the city's railway prospects still seemed bright, Oliver resurrected his notion of publishing a paper, and in that summer returned from Winnipeg with a $4 second-hand press. By the year's end, the *Bulletin* was born, and through it Frank Oliver became one of the leading spokesmen of the new West. In 1905, after twenty-two years in regional and federal politics, he was appointed to succeed Clifford Sifton as minister of the interior in the boom-time of western immigration.

its one type size was a tiny six point and each of its four pages measured a minuscule five inches wide by six inches deep – "the world's smallest newspaper," Oliver bragged.

But the editing-publishing team of Thomas Spink and Fitzgerald Cochrane of the Prince Albert *Times and Saskatchewan Review* was put to the most severe test. They and their party, which included four women, three children, seven white men, five Indians and several tons of presses, departed from Winnipeg by river boat on August 24, 1882. The first day out their steamer, lurching under the weight of the presses, ran aground on a sandbar. The captain released the boat and promptly returned to the Winnipeg docks where he dumped the newspaper team and their whole entourage.

Spink and Cochrane set out again, this time aboard a York boat, an open craft that the crew towed along the banks of the river using ropes and muscle power. The boat's skipper decided that his passengers would have to assume responsibility for loading and unloading their formidably heavy presses. "Steam boat companies take your money," Cochrane wrote in the second issue of his *Times*, "and don't seem to care what becomes of you or your freight." The group did not reach Prince Albert until October 25 – in time to make up the paper's first issue on November 1.

a virtual monopoly

A number of these pioneering newsmen had first learned their craft in Winnipeg. William Luxton and John Kenny, owners of the *Manitoba Free Press* from its beginnings in 1872, held a virtual monopoly in the West's early years. The *Free Press* could afford to hire a large staff and, in the early eighties, to purchase an American press capable of turning out in a single hour an incredible 1,800 copies of an eight-page paper printed on

one side. But the *Free Press* also distributed newspapermen across the West. George Ham went from the *Free Press* to set up the first news sheet in Edmonton in 1879, and beleaguered Fitzgerald Cochrane of the Prince Albert *Times* had learned his early skills in Winnipeg. Frank Oliver had served his apprenticeship on the *Free Press*, and received his miniature press and six-point type as a farewell gift from Messrs. Luxton and Kenny.

a one-man operation

The prairie papers, essentially one-man operations, reflected the varying personalities of their editor-publishers. Frank Oliver of the Edmonton *Bulletin* was a moralist, a *cheerful* sort of moralist, it was true, but still a man with a keen eye for sin, and he filled his paper with finger-wagging lectures to his fellow citizens. C.E.D. Wood and E.T. Saunders, on the other hand, took on the role of literary journalists in their Fort Macleod *Gazette*. Apart from current news, it offered jokes that were witty in a brittle drawing-room manner; a column of social notes with a cosmopolitan title, "In Town and Out"; a page of light literature; and a consistently popular feature – a serialized novel.

W.J. White of the Brandon *Mail* believed in sensationalism. One page of the September 11, 1884, issue included stories headed "Fisherman's Perils" (four sailors drown in Atlantic near Grand Banks), "A Domestic Drama" (absconding Ontario salesman-husband tracked down by wife) and "A Horrible Case of Cannibalism" (two shipwrecked sailors eat third in south Atlantic). White seemed convinced that *anything* foreign made better copy than domestic news. In the issue he published immediately after the outbreak of the Riel Rebellion, he dealt with the fighting at Duck Lake in an item on page eight headed "The Trouble Said to be of Grave Importance." But his editorial in the same issue examined at exhausting length the possible repercussions of a Russian attack on Afghanistan. The *Mail's* only consistent local feature, apart from its regular attacks on the owners of Winnipeg's *Free Press* whose Liberal politics White abhorred, was the column on page one in every issue devoted to the good works of Brandon's branch of the Woman's Christian Temperance Union.

Patrick Gammie Laurie may have been the *Free Press's* most illustrious alumnus. "Laurie was almost a heroic figure," wrote John Hawkes, an early Territories settler, "an able and courageous man, and the father of the press of Saskatchewan and Alberta." Laurie's Saskatchewan *Herald*, published from Battleford, became in 1878 the Territories' first newspaper, and in appearance, style and editorial philosophy the *Herald* set the tone for the other western papers. Throughout its pages, the *Herald* consistently reflected their one major preoccupation – the progress and status of their own prairie country. Western editors turned especially touchy when they dealt with the East's opinion of their people. All of them, most notably Laurie, scoured the "foreign" press – the papers of the U.S. and eastern Canada – for slanders.

grievances and prejudices

"The champion liar of the day lives in Ottawa," Laurie fulminated against Macdonald in one editorial, "and furnishes the United States with what purports to be news about 'Indian ravages' in the North West Territories." Laurie and his fellow editors felt that the Indians' troublesome ways were holding back western development and that the East took a far too unrealistic view of the lot of prairie tribes. Western papers were filled with editorials and letters ticking off grievances and complaints against the Indians, and their emotions soared in intensity after the 1885 uprising.

For all Laurie's apparent prejudices and paro-

PRAIRIE PAPERS

Flamboyant editor Nicholas Flood Davin (in top hat), staff and a newsboy at the false-front offices of the Regina Leader. *Below, Calgary* Herald *founders, Tom Braden (right) and Andrew Armour (left).*

THE TRIAL OF LOUIS RIEL

The scene is a crowded Regina courtroom on July 20, 1885. In the prisoner's box sits Louis Riel, leader of the Métis and Indian rebellion; in the jury box, the cold faces of six English-speaking jurors; among prosecutor Britton Bath Osler's witnesses, nearly a dozen men, themselves rebels, all charged with treason-felony; on the bench, Hugh Richardson, a judge reputed to have "no backbone." That Riel is guilty of inciting the rebellion is not the question. The charge is treason, and the Crown will have to prove that the man whom thousands regarded as the defender of their rights was in fact an enemy of the people, and knew right from wrong. September 18, 1885, the magistrate reads the death sentence. The trial is over.

Principal witnesses (l to r): W. Tomkins, Niss, Ross, Nolin, P. Tomkins, Wastley, Jackson and Sanderson. Some of the men called to the stand were themselves Métis charged with treason-felony.

The prisoner, Louis 'David' Riel, hurt his own best defence by claiming he was not insane.

The jury (l to r): Cosgrove (foreman), Merryfield, Brooks, Deane, Painter and Watt. Although the defendant could challenge the choice, in N.W.T. law, he was not allowed a bilingual jury.

chialism, he provided brave and resourceful coverage of the Riel Rebellion. Battleford, nestled at the junction of the Saskatchewan and Battle Rivers, was a supply centre for eight Indian reserves in the area – including the tribes led by Red Pheasant, Skinny Man, Mosquito and Poundmaker. When Riel's uprising lit the prairies, restless braves from the eight reserves under Poundmaker's banner swept down on Battleford. The townspeople, including Laurie, took refuge in the Mounted Police compound and stayed there for nearly four weeks, from March 30 to April 24, while the Indians looted and destroyed their homes and businesses. When a force under N.W.M.P. Superintendent Herchmer finally chased off Poundmaker's braves, Laurie emerged from the compound (where he'd taken a leading role in organizing the Battleford Home Guard) to find his entire plant wrecked – except for his precious press. Four days later, on April 28, working under more trying conditions than ever, Laurie turned out a four-page edition of the *Herald*. A headline reading "Battleford Beleaguered" stretched across a front page entirely devoted to an exhaustively detailed account, in diary form, of Battleford's perils during the Indian siege.

"a mass of rumors"

Laurie kept printing through May and most of June, although he had no advertisers, since there wasn't any business worth advertising in Battleford as long as the fighting lasted; but after the May 4 issue, economics forced him to cut down to a single two-page sheet. Acknowledging the problem of acquiring accurate information, Laurie headed many of his stories with the note of caution, "The Facts Sifted From a Mass of Rumors," and he frequently had to apologize for an earlier false report. Any *Herald* article credited "From Our Special Correspondent" invariably was based on

information furnished by a Laurie acquaintance like "Mr. Scott, the mail station master at Duck Lake." With this kind of help Laurie succeeded in publishing a series of war reports of remarkable scope and accuracy. The *Herald* dated May 11 offered a long and passionately convincing account of the battle at Cut Knife Creek, 38 miles outside of Battleford. Poundmaker turned back a 319-man force of militia and Mounties under Lt.-Col. Otter after seven hours of desperate fighting. Laurie's report, direct from Cut Knife, didn't miss a shot.

the hanging of Louis Riel

Throughout this virtuoso reporting display, Laurie never concealed his own emotional convictions. "Our great mistake [in 1870] was that we did not hang Riel," he wrote in a typical editorial comment on May 18. "Let not history repeat itself." On November 23, 1885, he began his report of the hanging of Louis Riel with this line: "The news of Riel's death was received here with satisfaction . . . " On November 27, when a coroner was needed to supervise the hanging of several Indians for their part in the Frog Lake massacre during the rebellion, the governor of the Territories didn't hesitate over his choice – Patrick Gammie Laurie.

Opinions - and prejudices - were publicly expressed, in strong language, not only by newspaper editors but also by politicians, men of the cloth – everyone. But the one point most Canadians *were* agreed upon when the North–West Rebellion first broke out was that the country should not tolerate violence, for whatever cause. A militia army, 8,000 strong, was raised from all the provinces. Montreal rallied to the cause of the Dominion as loyally and enthusiastically as any Canadian town or city. It dispatched the 65th Regiment, the Garrison Artillery and the Prince of Wales Rifles to help put down the insurrectionists. Bishop Fabre set aside

**Patrick Gammie Laurie
First Newsman in the N.W.T.**

From his appearance, one could easily mistake him for the clergyman his father was, but when it came down to hammering out a scathing editorial, Patrick Laurie was a firebrand. He was born in Scotland in 1833, came to Canada as a child, and was educated in Coburg, C.W. Before going west, he published papers in Owen Sound and Essex. As editor of the *Nor'-Wester* at Fort Garry in 1869, he had to flee for his life for refusing to print the pronouncements of Riel's provisional government. Like other pioneer journalists, he lugged his press by ox-cart from Winnipeg. But he started the Saskatchewan *Herald* in 1878 in the N.W.T. capital, Battleford. During the North-West Rebellion of 1885, except for the four weeks Battleford was besieged, Laurie continued to publish detailed accounts of events in two-page issues of the *Herald*. He is still known as the father of the press in Saskatchewan and Alberta.

April 17 as a day of penitence, fasting and prayer on behalf of the troops.

When the men returned in July, the city turned out *en masse* to greet them. The crowd reserved its warmest reception for the men of the 65th. They wore tattered, faded and soiled uniforms, and their heads were covered with every sort of gear, from cowboy hats to Indian feathers. But they were the troops who had seen the heaviest fighting – and they were French Canadians. In honour of the 65th, a band played "Vive La Canadienne," the bells of Notre Dame pealed and flags flew from every window. The regiment and the welcoming throng marched arm in arm to the Parish Church and together they sang the *Te Deum*.

But the mood of triumph and pride shared by English and French Montrealers rapidly faded. In its place an atmosphere of tension spread in thickening layers over the city as it became evident that Riel would hang. The social and racial differences that French and English had buried in times of mutual civic accomplishment rose to the surface.

The evening of Riel's execution, four hundred French Canadian students paraded through the downtown streets of Montreal carrying the Tricolour draped in black and singing "La Marseillaise." They stopped only once in the course of their parade – to burn Sir John A. in effigy. Next day an editorial in *La Presse* spoke for the students and probably for many other French Canadians in the city. "Henceforth," it said, "there are no more Conservatives nor Liberals nor Castors. There are only *PATRIOTS* and *TRAITORS* – the National Party and the Party of the Rope."

On the following Sunday, November 22, Mont-

real learned precisely how many of its citizens shared that emotion. Forty thousand people flocked to the greatest mass meeting in the city's history to protest the death of Riel, their compatriot. They gathered at the Champ de Mars in mid-morning and stayed through the afternoon. They cheered and roared for their own speakers and they jeered every mention of Macdonald's government. They heard thirty speakers; at some periods three speakers were holding forth at once.

Every faction of French-Canadian political thought was represented on the platforms and all the speakers repeated a single sentiment. Wilfrid Laurier for the Liberals declared, "If I had been on the banks of the Saskatchewan, I, too, would have shouldered my musket." Senator F.X.A. Trudel, an extreme right-wing ultramontane, compared Riel to Jesus and Joan of Arc. But it was Honoré Mercier who sparked the crowd's wildest ovation – and almost assured himself of the leadership of French Canada. Mercier, a journalist, lawyer and Liberal politician who championed an ardent brand of Quebec nationalism, seized the audience with his opening words. "Riel, our brother, is dead, victim of his devotion to the cause of the Métis of whom he was the leader, victim of fanaticism and treason" – and he never let them out of his grasp. "In killing Riel," Mercier harangued, "Sir John has struck not only a blow at the heart of our race, but above all he struck the cause of justice and humanity."

When French Montrealers returned home to the east end that night, the split between them and their fellow citizens, the English and Scots of the west side, seemed a little wider, a little more visible.

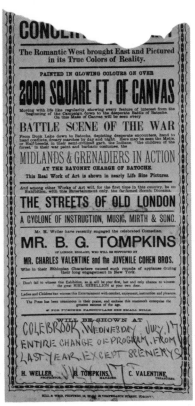

Before the advent of moving pictures and newsreels, sensational events such as the North-West Rebellion were "brought to life" mechanically. This poster announcing a gigantic diorama (painted scenes on canvas, animated through oscillating back-lights) is an incredible sample of eighties' show-biz.

Ladies and gentlemen of the French press visited Manitoba's Stony Mountain Penitentiary in 1886 to interview Cree chief Poundmaker. One of the great military strategists of the Indians, Poundmaker surrendered after Riel's capture, served one year in prison, and died shortly after his release.

REBELLION IN THE NORTH~WEST

Affairs in the North-West had become "so scandalously mismanaged by Eastern politicians" that local Métis and white settlers combined to raise the money to bring Louis Riel back from the U.S. in 1884 to present their grievances to the Dominion government. But Ottawa dithered. By February 1885, Riel's vision of himself as "David," a prophet for his people, had alienated the Church, and talk of armed force repelled white settlers. Not wanting violence, but supported by two competent "generals," Gabriel Dumont and Poundmaker, the unstable Riel proclaimed a provisional government and demanded the surrender of Ft. Carlton. Subsequent skirmishes with the Mounties and settlers and the first militia forces saw the Métis and Indians in virtual control of the area by the end of April. But Macdonald, speeding militia reinforcements to Major-General Middleton via the CPR, had no thought of giving in. By May 15, Riel had surrendered, and Dumont escaped to the U.S. With Poundmaker's surrender on May 26 and Big Bear's on July 2, the North-West Rebellion was over, but the political backlash was just beginning.

Fish Creek, April 24: Gabriel Dumont's ambush effectively halted Middleton's troops, en route to Riel's headquarters at Batoche.

After his success at Cut Knife Hill, Poundmaker set out for Batoche, only to hear of Riel's surrender. He then surrendered to Middleton at Battleford on May 26.

At the Amos Kinsey property at Cannington Manor, the fine team and rig had replaced the Red River cart (background) abandoned to the weeds beside the cabin.

CHAPTER FOUR

THE CURIOUS TRAIL THROUGH CANNINGTON MANOR

Where far from the shade and shelter of wood
The prairie hen rears her speckled brood.

Nicholas Flood Davin, "A Prairie Year"

By the standards the world uses to judge a man, Captain Edward Michell Pierce's life was a brave failure. At one time he owned a rambling mansion in the English countryside of Somersetshire, stood firmly for the Church and Army, and occupied a secure position in English trade and society. But in 1882 he suffered what he delicately referred to as "a financial setback." More plainly put, the captain went broke. Rather than face the humiliation of approaching his fine friends for help, he set out to make a new home for his wife, four daughters and four sons in the empty Canadian prairies.

Near Moose Mountain in southeast Saskatchewan, Captain Pierce established a settlement that resembled his former English estate. He advertised in London papers for "people of my own standing who wish to live like Princes on the little money they have and which would go in rates and taxes at home." So they came, remittance men and down-and-out English gentility, and at Pierce's Cannington Manor, they made cricket games, fox hunting, stately balls and dressing for dinner the order of the day. They lived in style and left the farming to hired hands. "I was glad when the young gentlemen took to tennis," one recalled, "so I could get on with the work."

The flowering of Cannington Manor on the prairies was typical of the crazy pattern of western settlement in the prairies. The 1881 census recorded a mere 56,446 white people living in the vast North-West Territories and 65,954 in Manitoba. It wasn't until the 1890s that the solid folk who eventually settled the west in great numbers began to trickle in. Through most of the eighties, the oddballs, the misfits, the adventurers, and the dispossessed arrived in the West, singly or in ready-made colonies of thousands.

At the beginning of the decade, Ottawa had mounted a lavish campaign in Europe extolling the opportunities on the prairies. All a man had to do was keep a 160-acre section of land under cultivation for three straight years and it was his, a no-strings gift from the Dominion. But word spread among potential immigrants that a few dry seasons in the late 1870s and two years of grasshopper invasion had made prairie farming a dicey proposition. Besides, the free homestead lands still available in the American West were more readily accessible – the Northern Pacific Railway had reached Bismarck, North Dakota, as early as 1873 and Miles City, Montana, by 1881.

Until the CPR finally marched across the prairie, settlers had to rely on shanks's mare to reach their land. "We walked ninety miles in search of homestead sites," one settler reported from Manitoba in 1881, "but returned unsatisfied.

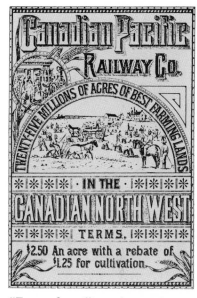

"Twenty-five millions of acres of best farming lands" was part of the subsidy to induce the syndicate to build the CPR. Twenty-five millions in cash went along with the land. The syndicate's commitment was to build and operate the main line "efficiently." To discourage speculators, the CPR offered rebates to buyers who actually farmed the land.

**Captain E. M. Pierce
Squire of Cannington Manor**

A little bit of England transplanted to the Canadian prairie flourished briefly in the '80s and '90s. When Edward Michell Pierce secured homestead acreage forty miles from Moosomin for himself and his four sons in 1882, he called the area Cannington Manor–perhaps to remind himself of his former estate in England. There never was a manor; in fact with his log house under construction, the Captain spent his first winter in the cellar. But by the next summer, his home, including the "college" for his agricultural pupils, was the focus of a growing, self-sustained community. The young Englishmen who undertook the farming lessons were even more enthusiastic participants in the cultural and social life organized by the families of the Manor. The Captain did not have to witness the eventual demise of the village, for he died in 1888.

In spring I bought a team of oxen, two carts and some equipment, and my brother and I set out walking 120 miles northwest from Winnipeg."

the sod house

A series of linking trails serviced the prairies: the Carlton Trail, winding west from Winnipeg deep into the North-West Territories; the Melita Trail, slicing through Manitoba's interior; the Old North Trail, joining Calgary to Edmonton. But they were little more than parallel ruts sunk deep in the prairie mud, wandering perversely through water-filled sloughs, plunging ravines and streams wide and deep enough to make a man unload and reload his wagon half a dozen times a day to save his supplies from a drenching. The trails took their toll in many ways. "Even if there had been no trail," Gerald Willoughby wrote, describing a harrowing journey along the route out of Moose Jaw in April 1883, "a stranger could have found his way into the north country by the bones of the horses that died by the way."

The first home that most prairie farmers knew was made from sod, often the only building material available. Settlers cut the sod – like over-sized bricks, three feet long by two feet wide and six inches thick – from a slough bottom where the grass roots were thick and tough, and they stacked them in tiers to a height of eight feet. The houses usually measured a modest twelve feet by eight or nine, relieved only by one lop-sided door and two windows, also lop-sided. The roof, too, was made of sod or light willow brush; both kinds had a property in common – they leaked.

Inside, a bolt of cloth served as partition; walls were lined with planks and whitewashed monthly (lime sold at twenty-five pounds for twenty-five cents). House-proud wives spread hooked rugs on the floor, which was either wood or earth depending on the owner's affluence and resourcefulness,

and covered the ceiling with white cotton. Everything else, apart from the inevitable *Family Herald* illustrations of the Royal Family tacked to the walls, was strictly utilitarian: home-made furniture, heavy white ironstone dishes, steel cutlery, black iron cooking pots and a copper kettle. The pride of the house, and usually the only item of store-bought furnishings, was a square, squat, wood-burning, cast-iron stove with a trade name like The Homesteader or The Rancher or The Grand Jewel. Every day the lady of the sod-house gave it a determined rub with Dome or Rising Sun black lead polish to keep it, of all her possessions, gleaming with a high shine.

daily rituals

Each household chore brought built-in obstacles that guaranteed elaborate and time-eating labour. Washing clothes was a complex businesss because the hard well-water of the prairies curdled the soap. The steel cutlery required constant scouring with ashes or sand and, for a decent shine, an extra rub with powder scraped from a bar of bathbrick. Cleaning the chimneys or the coal-oil lamps, sweeping the earth floor after first laying the dust with damp tea leaves, gathering fuel for the stove (buffalo chips or straw twists when wood was scarce), baking bread, cooking– all these devoured time and energy in a grinding daily ritual.

"Just the whole long process of looking after the milk was a continuous chore," Mrs. Isabel Reekie remembered from her days on a farm near the Melita Trail. She had to milk the cows, strain the milk into pans, set them to cool in a dugout cellar, skim the cream, store it in a crock for churning, wash the utensils, scald them and set them away until the next milking. A prairie wife developed iron biceps, just from churning the butter. But she needed those biceps because prairie men expected their women also to help them look after the livestock and bring in the crops.

The clothes the homesteaders wore were notable only for their practical ordinariness. For men, duck or denim pants and jackets, hand-sewn boots, white shirts only for Sunday-best. For women, blue-indigo denim dresses with body lining and tucked fronts, voluminous aprons gathered on a wide band flowing into strings, flannel bloomers with cotton strips over the seams to cut down the itch, and a sunbonnet. "To get dressed, buttonhooks were a gadget you had to own," Agnes Haight recalled from her homesteading experiences in Manitoba. "Our shoes were high buttoned. We wore waists made from bleached flour bags with buttons on the side. There were even buttons on our stockings."

For plain homeliness, the prairie diet easily matched prairie clothing. Salt pork was a day-after-day staple; fresh meat and fresh fruit and vegetables were rare on western tables. Housewives relied on bread and butter, oatmeal, grits, potatoes, corn syrup, dried peas and beans, and eggs in summer. "Long clear bacon, 12¢ a pound," read a grocer's advertisement in the *Manitoba Free Press* in the spring of 1887, "16 pounds of coffee, $1: sugar, 5¢ a pound; 100-pound bag of flour, $2.90 to $3.75; raisins, 10 to 13¢ a pound; evaporated apples, 9 pounds for $1."

wild sage and onions

Of necessity, homesteaders looked to the land to yield the mild gourmet touches for their meals. The men hunted rabbits and game birds, fished the streams and searched the hills for berry bushes. The women could be more enterprising. "We gathered wild sage and onions for seasoning," wrote Maryanne Carswell of her childhood on a farm near Saskatoon, "and tansy and yarrow for yeast. We also collected golden-rod for dye, worm-

Cannington Manor racecourse, the best in the west, was started in 1887 for the Queen's Jubilee.

Manorites donned their best for Hunt Club activities and social events like the LeMesurier wedding.

A NEW LIFE

The CPR's route change in 1881 caused boom-or-bust times for settlements in the southwestern prairie, but along the old Carlton Trail that traders had followed from Manitoba northwest to Edmonton, new arrivals trickled in and set about with a determined spirit to re-establish their version of the amenities of civilization.

Right: Settlers in the beautiful Qu'Appelle Valley district dressed up for a day of visiting friends or neighbours.

Below: In 1881, Edmontonians determined that their hamlet of about 300 souls should have its first permanent school.

wood for use as poultices to reduce swelling, and anise with its long, purple, licorice-odoured spikes for cough medicine."

Hospitality, when an opportunity for it arose, was overwhelming in its warmth. A man who dropped in on his neighbour (anyone who lived within forty miles) expected to stay for three or four days. His host was disappointed and insulted if he did not. Families organized a regular exchange of papers and books. Tattered copies of western papers (*Manitoba Weekly Free Press, Western Home Monthly, Nor'West Farmer*) and magazines *(Good Words, Sunday at Home)* passed among homesteaders until they were crumpled beyond legibility.

At agricultural fairs, at weddings and dances, prairie socializing took on a determined, even desperate, intensity. Couples would drive their carts thirty miles or more through any weather for a dance, held in a barn cleared for the occasion or in a community hall erected by the homesteaders. To music provided by a single heroic fiddler or mouth organ player, they danced until sunrise, pounding and shaking the earth in hardy western versions of military or Highland schottisches, heel and toe polkas or square dances.

a sense of humour

All prairie entertainment – bachelor picnics, evenings of community whist or euchre, the occasional dash of eastern-style show business – was manifestly do-it-yourself. "We had our Social Evenings," wrote Mrs. Willey of the Sumner Colony, "where everyone did the stunt that was expected of him. Mr. Sumner sang "Old Dan Tucker" and another ditty about an old man 'who was as cunning as a fox and who always had tobacco in his old tobacco box.' The choruses we all sang, and here I first heard "Clementine", "My Bonnie" and "Wrap Me Up In My Tarpaulin

Jacket" – who introduced them is shrouded in mystery, but we always sang them!" To many settlers, these efforts at liveliness were an essential defence against the harshness of their predicament. "We learned to depend on our own resources," Mrs. Harold Bateman wrote of her pioneer life in southwestern Manitoba, "but nothing at all counted for much if you didn't have a good sense of humour and lots of patience."

seeking the ideal life

It wasn't surprising that Ottawa's early efforts at promoting western settlement appealed mainly to groups and organizations with especially *anxious* reasons for exchanging their situations in Europe or in eastern Canada for the rugged existence of the prairies – Jews fleeing the pogroms in Russia, Cockneys escaping poverty in London slums, Mormons avoiding the American government's anti-polygamy laws, Hungarian romantics seeking some mysterious ideal life, Ontario businessmen with plans for turning a fast buck by streamlining farming into a productive new industry, temperance advocates looking for a liquor-less haven, English gentlemen who visualized virgin fox-hunting country on the prairies.

The first Jewish community began to take root in the West when the Coblentz brothers, Edmond, Aachel and Adolphe, of Philadelphia, moved to Manitoba in 1879. They were talented, adaptable, gregarious fellows, fluent in English, French, Hebrew and German, and they quickly made themselves popular citizens of frontier Manitoba. Adolphe opened the Golden Hotel in East Lynne, Edmond and Aachel went into the drygoods business in and around Winnipeg, and more Jews followed on their success. The 1881 census recorded thirty-three Jewish people living in the Winnipeg area alone.

Sir Alexander Tilloch Galt, Canada's High

The first permanent Jewish settlers in the Winnipeg area, the Coblentz brothers, Edmond, Aachel and Adolphe, came from Alsace-Lorraine via Philadelphia in the late seventies. On January 28, 1879, a child was born to Adolphe and his wife. By 1881 there were thirty-three Jewish families in the province of Manitoba.

Commissioner in London, was responsible for multiplying their number several hundred-fold. Galt joined the Archbishop of Canterbury and several titled English gentlemen on the London Mansion Committee in 1881 to aid victims of Russia's sudden and savage anti-Semitic pogrom. His suggestion of Manitoba as a generous refuge was taken up, and, in May 1882, 350 nearly penniless Jewish immigrants reached Winnipeg. At first the prairies struck the new arrivals as a fate worse than a pogrom. One immigrant painted a heart-breaking picture in a letter to *Hamelitz,* the leading Hebrew publication in Russia.

I know not in what to dip my pen, in the inkstand before me, or in the flow of tears running from the eyes of the unfortunates who have come here with me, in order to describe their lamentable condition. One hears nothing but weeping and wailing over the prospect of wasting one's youth and spending it vainly in this desolation known as Winnipeg.

Manitoba's increase in population from 62,000 to 152,000 between 1881 and '91 was due not just to the extension of the province's boundaries but to an influx of immigrants attracted by glowing phrases in pamphlets like the one above for potential Dutch farmers.

pioneer conditions

Many of the refugees eventually found their way into various trades and businesses, but a few Jewish families attempted to establish agricultural colonies, a task for which their previous experiences in urban ghettos did not guarantee success. One colony in Manitoba, called New Jerusalem, folded quickly; but Hirsch, in Saskatchewan, held on through the familiar grinding pioneer conditions. Even the disgruntled *Hamelitz* correspondent later wrote again to Russia:

Perhaps I somewhat exaggerated, but truthfully, our living conditions after our arrival were unendurable. We have gradually accustomed ourselves to the hard work . . . . Here, in this new country, even the cultured and the well-bred among us

have to discard our starched shirts and properly shined shoes, and have gotten down to work.

That young man's process of adjustment was swift compared to the unfortunate Hungarians from the settlement organized by Count Paul Esterhazy near the town of Whitewood in southeast Saskatchewan. The Count was an elusive figure who may have been a commoner and an impostor named John Papp, but he did have every good intention of recreating for several hundred Hungarian immigrants a gay, prosperous slice of old Budapest in the West.

creating a colony

The Count appointed his friend Julian Vass as postmaster and director of the colony. But Vass was, in the words of John Hawkes, a pioneer farmer who lived forty miles down the line from the Hungarians, "a man of education and refinement, perhaps thirty-five years of age, prematurely bald, a good-looking, easy-going, pleasant-mannered fellow who had every qualification except the important one of business ability. . . . His lack of business capacity, combined with a somewhat pleasure-loving disposition, led to disaster. He became involved, and shot himself to death in a Walpella hotel to the great regret of a large circle of friends." Despite such misfortunes added to the drought and prairie fires, the colony kept going. In later years the settlement blossomed into a busy town as more Hungarian immigrants arrived in Canada – along with Slovak, Croat, Serbian and Czech newcomers – and found their way to the area with the friendly-sounding name, Esterhazy.

The band of Mormons who trekked into the Lee's Creek district of southern Alberta in the spring of 1887 approached settlement on the prairie with intelligence and organization. They arrived on the run from the recently promulgated laws forbidding polygamy in the United States. But the Mormon men were clear-thinking enough to enter the new country, which might also prove touchy on the marriage question, with just one wife apiece. And they set about the job of creating a colony with remarkable discipline. They irrigated the land, built a grist mill and a saw mill, and they established themselves as the principal suppliers of butter, eggs and vegetables to nearby Fort Macleod and Lethbridge.

Many Canadians were warily fascinated by Mormon marriage practices. The Edmonton *Bulletin* labelled them "undesirables," the Montreal *Star* called for their exclusion from Canada and, in his 1888 Annual Report to the prime minister, Commissioner Herchmer of the N.W.M.P. expressed his reservations about Mormon morals. "They are, so far as progress and enterprise go, the very best settlers in our country, but any attempt to introduce the practice of polygamy under any guise must be promptly dealt with."

settling in to stay

The criticism didn't bother the Mormons. Their leader, Charles Card, whose one wife in Canada was the daughter of Brigham Young, journeyed to Ottawa and asked the prime minister for the use of timber resources, for the sale of some low-priced land and for permission to import the Mormon wives left behind in Utah. Sir John responded by amending the Criminal Code to make polygamy, previously ignored by Canadian legislation and therefore presumably permissible in Canada, a federal offence. But the Mormons continued to prosper; they accumulated enough savings to purchase, at a dollar an acre, half a million acres of land; they changed the name of Lee's Creek to Cardston in honour of their leader; and they settled in to stay.

The federal government responded far more

By the summer of 1887, forty-one Mormon colonists under their leader Charles Card had made a permanent settlement in southern Alberta. Here one group enjoys a bounteous picnic.

One of the major colonization plans for the prairies brought the Bell Farm into existence near Indian Head, Saskatchewan. Major Wm. R. Bell, an Ontario businessman, organized the nine-mile-square farm and oversaw its ambitious operation. Ultimately the Bell Farm was obliged to close down but its farm workers contributed to the development of the prairies. From this photo, the Major appears to have been a member of the Shriners.

generously with aid to groups of Ontario and English businessmen than it did to the Mormons. In the early 1880s, in an effort to fill up some of the West's empty spaces, Ottawa handed over large chunks of land at bargain-basement prices to colonization companies with the stipulation that the companies place a minimum of 128 settlers on each township they received. The companies proved sadly inadequate to the task, as the minister of the interior discovered at meetings in the fall of 1884. The Montreal & Western Land Company had managed to settle a mere 64 homesteaders on its 24,580 acres; the Primitive Methodist Colony had 104 settlers on 36,000 acres; the York Farmers Colonization Company showed 164 settlers on 51,358 acres; the Temperance Colony at Saskatoon, 101 settlers on 100,000 acres; and there were other companies with even grimmer records.

an invaluable legacy

The most colossal venture at commercial settlement and farming, likewise a failure, was the Bell Farm at Indian Head in Saskatchewan. Its founder was a tall, imposing, noble-spirited Ontario businessman named Major William Bell. "Clad in knightly armour, or possibly without it," wrote John Hawkes, "Major Bell would have tilted with a light heart and a steady hand at all comers." In 1883 he purchased from the Dominion and the CPR a huge tract of land said to measure nine miles square, the largest farm of continuous land in the world. The Major equipped the farm in appropriately Brobdingnagian style; he built a sixteen-room stone house, two grain elevators, flour mills, and a magnificent circular stone barn, forty-five feet in diameter, and he stocked the land with 250 head of cattle and 900 hogs. By 1886 he had 5,000 acres in crop, maintained by 45 reapers and binders, 73 ploughs, 40 seeders, 80 sets of harrows, and a staff of more than 200 farmhands from the East.

But every circumstance seemed to work against Bell Farm. There was a disastrous early frost in 1884. The next year Major Bell dispatched much of his labour force and a hundred teams of horses to help put down Riel, and he planted no crop that year. The year after that there was a drought and in 1888 the farm's creditors swooped down. Major Bell was forced to close his farm, but, when he moved to Bermuda, he left behind him hundreds of skilled farm workers, in addition to his mills, elevators and other equipment, an invaluable legacy to the young prairie country.

"young and full of life"

The charitable colonization organizations turned out to be more durable than the commercial companies because they were less ambitious in size and because they were usually bankrolled by wealthy and mildly eccentric British ladies of title. Lady Gordon Cathcart selected a group of crofters from her estates in Scotland and set them down in the Moosomin area of southeast Saskatchewan in 1883. They adjusted to their new environment with satisfying ease and speed. The London Cockneys whom Baroness Burdett-Coutts settled in the same district a year later didn't immediately make out as successfully. "The experiment has been tried of bringing out East Londoners," reported an American journalist Charles Dudley Warner who was touring the west on assignment for *Harper's Magazine*. "These barbarians of civilization are about as unfitted for colonists as [they] can be." But Warner was too hasty in his judgement. The Cockneys needed only time; in 1888, of the original twenty families the Baroness sent west, twelve were still on their farms, five had moved to Moosomin where the men worked at small crafts, and only three were unaccounted for.

The most engaging settlement group was the crowd at Captain Edward Pierce's Cannington

Manor. Their cricket games and fox hunts and black-tie dinners made them totally atypical, but their buoyant good spirits and their confidence that they would somehow conquer that trying landscape exemplified the finest mood of all the settlers who stayed to carve out a new life in the western prairies.

"It was all such a change from our luxurious life in England," wrote Captain Pierce's eldest daughter Lily, "but we were young and full of life, had the great joy of being all together, and everything seemed a joke and so we were very happy. . . . There were enough for players for two cricket teams and many an exciting match we had. We had tennis, football and fox hunting, all the dancing we wanted, and parties and entertainments to our hearts' content."

They also managed, at least occasionally, to fit in time for farming and building. Captain Pierce hired farming instructors and took on young English pupils at $500 per year. The young novices absorbed enough lore to win a gold medal for an exhibit of flour at the Paris Exposition in 1889. The community built a fine log house for Captain Pierce's family, a general store, a flour mill, a school house and a church, Anglican of course.

But, more than anything tangible, the Manor contributed to the west an emotion, a feeling of joy. "We had a very good class of people in and around Cannington," a N.W.M.P. sergeant wrote in the late 1890s. "Most of them had a remittance, a jolly good time, a pack of hounds – and to hang with the farm." His words remain a fine and fitting epitaph.

Davis, T. O., Prince Albert, rt. h.

Foster, Nelson, Lipton, rt. f.

Huffman, A. M., East End, rt. sh.

Allen, T. C., Medicine Hat, Alta., l. th.

Preece, John, Preeceville, l. th.

Gillespie, Andrew G., McDonald Hills, rt. th.

Gibson, W. Thomas, Coulee, l. sh. (vent bar through br'nd)

McDonald, J. H., Belanger, rt. sh.

Kearney, R. A., G. E., & J. C., Maple Creek, l. sh.

Hassett, Will A. Blenner, Maple Creek, rt. th.

Jahn, B. A., Battle Creek, l. th.

Gilchrist, Reuben, Battle Creek, l. th.

Markham, W. H., Crescent Lake, rt. sh.

Huckvale, Walter, Medicine Hat, Alta., l. th.

Registered brands of ranchers in the Alberta and Saskatchewan districts.

Not everyone who moved west in the eighties wanted to homestead. This decade also saw the beginning of the brief era of sprawling cattle ranches in the foothills of southern Alberta. In 1881 Sen. M.H. Cochrane of Que. secured a grazing lease on 100,000 acres west of Calgary at a yearly rental of one cent an acre and acquired 3,000 head of cattle from Montana. True to its name, his British America Ranch Co. combined the wild cowboy style of the American West with the polo-playing, riding-to-hounds customs of the English. At left, a "group of wealthy hunters" at the ranch. The woman on the right shows off the latest Paris fashion in hunting dress–a checked suit, its pleated skirt daringly knee-length.

CHAPTER FIVE

A SORRY NIGHT IN CHINATOWN

"Person" means a male person, including an Indian, and excluding a person of Chinese race.

Electoral Franchise Act, July 20, 1885

Locksley Lucas's pals used to say that in all of British Columbia no one could match his black temper or his silver tongue. Since Locksley's pals were a tough-minded, gabby bunch themselves, their estimation carried a lot of authority. Locksley and the others made their living as navvies – and like navvies all over the world in the last decades of the nineteenth century, they took their jobs wherever they could find them. In the 1880s they hired on with Andrew Onderdonk to build the CPR line through the mountains and wilderness of British Columbia. It was as tortuous a stretch of track as Locksley or anyone else had ever laid, but they got the job done – ahead of schedule. And in the last months of 1886, they moved down to Vancouver and put in their days sitting around saloons that offered five-cent schooners of beer to fill their stomachs, and pot-bellied stoves to drive the chill out of their bones.

Life passed pleasantly enough but there were, in fact, two things very wrong. First, hardly anybody – contractor, builder, engineer – was advertising work for navvies. Second, the bosses who *were* hiring favoured the Chinese communities in and around Vancouver. And as the days went on

with no prospect of work, Locksley Lucas had plenty to say about that. "Lucas was smooth-tongued, all right," William Findlay later recalled; (Findlay was a boy in the 1880s but knew Locksley as a resident of his uncle's hotel, the Carter House.) "He was a real agitator, and when they got together an organization to keep the Chinamen out of Vancouver for all time, they elected him treasurer. He collected a lot of money."

But Locksley took on a larger role than mere treasurer. When the navvies and some other Vancouver citizens rallied for an anti-Chinese demonstration outside the Sunnyside Hotel late in February, Locksley joined with several speakers in haranguing the crowd from the hotel verandah. He proved himself to be, indeed, a smooth-talking, black-tempered orator. His words helped drive his half-drunk navvy pals into a dumb frenzy. Under his and the others' malevolent influence, that February night burst into a horror of cruelty, destruction and spilled blood – Chinese blood.

By 1887, the white workers' fear of the Chinese had already been building in temper for thirty years – or ever since the first Chinese found their way to the Canadian West. These Asian pioneers were initially attracted to Canada by the prospect of trade in furs. Many of them fell immediately into the roles of laundrymen, cooks and servants. Some were labourers, some were fur traders and a few mined gold, though they confined their pros-

A. Onderdonk began hiring Chinese labourers in 1880, his first group coming from the Northern Pacific R.R. in Oregon. Then he began to charter sailing ships to bring in thousands of Chinese directly from Canton, the only port permitting foreign trade.

Opposite page: The Chinese were hired in large groups through agents who represented companies in Canton. The coolies organized into gangs of about thirty men, designating one man to act as bookman and deal directly with the white foreman. Paid a dollar a day each, the Chinese kept to themselves in camps like this one at Keefers station between Lytton and Boston Bar.

**Andrew Onderdonk
Master Builder**

"No such mountain work had ever been attempted in Canada before," said one observer, but Andrew Onderdonk, scion of an old New York family, took up the challenge and built the CPR through the formidable Fraser Canyon. Only thirty-one when awarded the contracts in 1879, he soon set up headquarters at Yale and took on work gangs to carry out the first stage–blasting twenty-seven tunnels out of the canyon rock. It was long, hard, dangerous work but Onderdonk's lambs, as his labourers were called, girded the walls of the foaming canyon with trestles and tunnels and cold steel tracks by 1885. Still an aloof and unassuming man, Onderdonk went on to build the Entre Rios Railroad in South America, came back to Canada to work on the Trent and Soulanges canals in 1895, then died at the age of fifty-six while building the subway tunnel under New York's East River in 1905.

pecting to areas the white miners had rejected. They had learned not to make themselves conspicuous in the neighbourhood of a Canadian with a colour prejudice and a gun.

It was left to Andrew Onderdonk to pitch the problem on a new, more dramatic plane. When he moved to British Columbia in 1880 to build the CPR line, he found every resource he needed except one – manpower. In all of British Columbia there weren't enough labourers and navvies to push the line of steel through the formidable western wilderness. Onderdonk turned to China; through the mid-1880s he imported ten thousand Chinese to build his railroad. And he saved money; Onderdonk later estimated that he cut pay-roll costs by twenty-five percent when he hired cheap Chinese labour instead of expensive navvies from Europe.

uneasy racial truce

As long as the CPR was in its building stage, an uneasy racial truce prevailed. The railway was essential to the province and the Chinese were essential to the railway. Besides, there were jobs for all. But the forced peace lasted only as long as the jobs did. In 1885 and 1886, as teams of workers completed their sections of the Onderdonk line, Chinese and whites began to flood back to the coast from the interior. "A thousand white men rushed out of the cars and into the saloons," reported the Port Moody *Gazette*, describing the day when a train-load of rail workers descended on Yale. "In two hours the streets were full of lunatics; they roared and raved and tried to force their way into private houses. Twelve hundred Chinese arrived by the same train, and went into the woods and cooked their rice."

Most of the men, white and Chinese, eventually headed for the country around Vancouver, a town that revelled in its frontier ruggedness. Gastown, as the area was first named in honour of

"Gassy" Jack Deighton, then Granville in tribute to a British colonial secretary, didn't begin to boom until it became Vancouver, the site selected by William Van Horne as the western terminus for the CPR. Van Horne reached his decision in the fall of 1884, and by April 6, 1886, the day Vancouver was incorporated, it boasted a dozen hotels, three restaurants, five groceries, four boot-and-shoe shops, a Chinese wash house, ten real-estate offices and a hard-drinking free-and-easy style of life. At Tom Cyr's Granville Hotel every guest was entitled to an eye-opener before breakfast, and by local custom in all the bars, no stranger in town rated a drink of his own until he'd stood the house a round. Most saloons peddled booze in two measures – a "short bit," one drink for ten cents, or a "long bit," six drinks for twenty-five cents.

The first, hastily built Vancouver didn't survive long after incorporation day. Citizens on their way to St. James' Church on Sunday morning, June 13, smelled smoke in the air, but they gave it little mind. The railroad men had been burning their land clear for days. And anyway, it was a soft warm lazy day, small sailboats were sweeping across the bay, families were packing for picnics on the North Shore, the old barque *Robert Kerr* was swinging gently back and forth in the inlet. Then suddenly, in the midst of the peaceful scene, about two o'clock in the afternoon, dense choking smoke began to pour into the streets. Vancouver was on fire.

the Vancouver fire

The flames swept through the dry wood buildings so fast that the town simply melted. "As an illustration of the heat," a survivor of the fire, William Gallagher, later recalled, "there was a man, driving horse and wagon, caught on Carrall Street. The man and the horse perished in the centre of the street. Two iron tires and some ashes

VANCOUVER

"Destined to be a great city," said William Van Horne of Granville on Burrard Inlet and he proposed a name "commensurate with its dignity." On April 6, 1886, the City of Vancouver was officially born. That June a fire devastated the small community but the citizens, about 1,000 strong by the summer, rebuilt quickly–brick and stone structures predominated–and by the year's end a thriving business centre was in operation and the CPR was constructing a depot and a wharf at Coal Harbour.

Vancouverites enjoying springtime in the 1,000-acre parkland set aside by Mayor M.A. Maclean's new city council and dedicated in 1889 as Stanley Park by the governor general for whom it was named.

The morning after the fire, tents pitched on still-warm ground served as temporary headquarters for relief work by Chief Stewart's stalwarts.

The little steamer Senator *ferried parties to social events in larger nearby towns. The man standing on the right (wearing top hat) is David Oppenheimer, the city's second mayor.*

CHINATOWN

The distinctive flavour that a Chinatown brought to the towns and cities of B.C. was not always viewed affectionately by the whites of the area. But there hadn't been many white settlers there when the first Chinese came, attracted by the fur trade and the gold rush. Like Onderdonk's labourers, these immigrants expected to return to China after making their "fortune." But some stayed on, sent home for wives, established families and businesses and withstood the often vociferous opposition.

Victoria as well as Vancouver had a street where Chinese families who had opted to stay in Canada congregated. They ran laundries and grocery stores serving both their own community and the whites.

The parents of these youngsters on Barkerville's main street may have reached the area during the Fraser gold rush.

Wah Chong, the older gentleman in the centre of the family group, had moved his laundry from Hastings townsite to Water Street near Carrall in Granville where this photo was taken in 1884.

was all that was left of man, horse and wagon." The fire whipped down the plank sidewalks faster than a man could run. It burned to death at least thirty citizens and it levelled the town. "Two thirds of the people of Vancouver the day after the fire," the Vancouver *Advertiser* wrote on June 29, "could not boast of more than the clothes they stood in."

But Vancouver recovered almost as quickly as it had been destroyed. Captain William Clements, who lost his Tremont Hotel to the flames, set up business the very next day, selling beer from an open-air bar fashioned out of a couple of planks supported by two empty kegs. George Allan had his shoe store half restored by three in the afternoon and the Reverend Thompson of the Presbyterian Church held a service in George's place before supper. "Take what you need," a sign announced at the Hastings sawmill; everyone did, and within three days, a dozen firms were back in operation in frame buildings.

the navvies hit town

By the time the railway men hit town, Vancouver was once again purveying long bits and five-cent schooners of beer. Every bar and saloon roared through the days and nights, and both newcomers and regulars had drunk themselves silly before twilight. Malcolm Maclean, Vancouver's first mayor, and his new chief constable, big bluff John Stewart, struggled manfully to keep the peace for the sake of Vancouver's growing population of law-abiding, God-fearing, family-raising citizens. Chief Stewart commanded a staff of three constables, each man freshly decked out in badge, blue serge and bobby's helmet.

But not even the London police force in all its might could have deterred the men in the saloons from their anti-Chinese ranting. The railroad navvies were outraged that the CPR had taken on almost exclusively Chinese labour to build the final twelve miles of track, the grade from Port Moody to Vancouver. And they nursed a dozen other grievances. Some navvies had arrived in Vancouver before the fire and had taken the only work they could find, sweating alongside Indians and Chinese for ten hours a day, $1.25 per day, at the Hastings sawmill. The whites struck for higher wages in April of 1886, but the mill manager, a man named Alexander, just threw them out and hired a few more Indians and Chinese.

threat of Chinese labour

The permanent Chinese residents of Vancouver lived in an area that whites instantly labelled Chinatown. It wasn't the most desirable section. "On the corner of Abbott and Cordova Streets was a row of Chinese cabins and some other occupants of ill repute," was the way William Gallagher described Chinatown. The flow of new immigrants from China into the area was drastically reduced when Sir John A. Macdonald, finally giving in to British Columbia's complaints, imposed a head tax of $50 per man on Chinese immigrants; the number of new Chinese dropped from four thousand to under a thousand in the later 1880s. As for the Chinese from Onderdonk's railroad, they lingered in Vancouver only long enough to calculate the temper of the whites. Then some drifted back into the British Columbia interior; many more crossed over to Victoria.

A Vancouver contractor named McDougall set out to bring them back. In the winter of 1886-87, McDougall won a contract from William Brighouse and Sam Hailstone, two big Vancouver landowners, to clear off their District Lot 185, about a mile west of town. He hired Chinese from Victoria to do the job, and that was the last straw for the navvies in the saloons and for many other Vancouverites. They took to meeting the Victoria

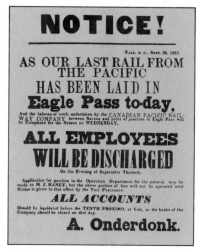

With the laying of the last rail from the Pacific on September 26, 1885, A. Onderdonk gave notice of discharge to all employees. The navvies, both whites and Chinese, flooded back to the Coast.

boats at the dock and, if they found Chinese passengers, they'd drive them back aboard for the return trip to Victoria. McDougall countered by smuggling his Chinese in by private night boats and eventually he organized a camp of two hundred workers in tents and shanties on the Lot.

The situation simmered and boiled amid grumbles, oaths, threats and promises of violence until deep into February 1887. On February 24, one of Locksley Lucas's cronies paraded through town carrying a placard that proclaimed "The Chinese have come. Mass meeting tonight in City Hall." There *was* a meeting that night, but Mayor Maclean, who wanted no part of the trouble, shooed the throng out of City Hall and down the street to the Sunnyside Hotel. There, booze and oratory took over. Lucas and the other speakers thundered their hatred of the Chinese – they were a threat to white men's pocket-books and the whites had to take the law into their own hands to meet the threat. The meeting passed resolutions condemning the Chinese, Sir John A. and the government in Victoria. Then, from out of the crowd, a loud voice cried, "Those in favour of turning out the Chinese tonight, shout 'aye'." A crashing AYE decided the matter and a mob of men set off for McDougall's camp shouting "Tonight, tonight" and singing "John Brown's Body" at the top of their lungs.

"Amidst howls and yells"

It was close to midnight, there was snow on the ground, and the Chinese could hear the whites coming when the mob was still a quarter mile away. They clung to the tent poles in terror, poked their heads out under the canvas flaps and waited. The white men charged into the clearing and, in the description of the *Daily News* on February 25, "Amidst howls and yells, they commenced the work of seizing the Chinamen."

Some Chinese fled from their tents. Some were dressed, some not, some wore shoes, most were barefoot. They just ran. "Perhaps in the darkness, they did not know about the cliff and the drop of twenty feet," William Gallagher later wrote; he joined the mob in an effort to prevent violence. "Perhaps some had forgotten, some may have lost direction. The tide was in. They had no choice, and you could hear them – *plump, plump, plump* – as they jumped into the salt water. Scores of them went over the cliff . . . . I have heard it said, that four Chinamen were tied by their pigtails and thrown into the creek."

a meagre bargain

Most of the whites confined themselves to kicking the Chinese, tearing down their shelters and ordering them back to Victoria, and they were still at their destructive games when Chief Stewart of the city police and Superintendent Raycroft of the Mounties finally showed up. The two officers sheltered the remaining Chinese in one partly wrecked shanty and persuaded the milling whites to return to town. It was three in the morning but none of the men felt ready for bed and all headed for the Sunnyside bar. They had a few rounds of drinks and they agreed that, next day, it was Chinatown's turn.

A few hours later, not long after eight o'clock, the navvies, the labourers, the disgruntled whites once again gathered in the street outside the Sunnyside. This time they'd brought transportation, about twenty-five drays and wagons. They were going to ship the Chinese out of Vancouver once and for all. The Chinese, for their part, had been up all night; some of them had been fighting a fire in their district, which they suspected a drunken white had set. And that morning they sent forward their senior merchants to bargain with the angry white men.

It was May 23, 1887, Queen Victoria's Jubilee year, when the new depot in Vancouver received its first transcontinental passenger train. More than 2,000 spectators cheered as the garlanded engine, with MONTREAL GREETS THE TERMINAL CITY emblazoned on its smokestack, provided a backdrop for dignitaries speaking eloquently of the great future in store for Vancouver.

The parley took until almost noon and in the end the Chinese elders won only a meagre bargain. The whites agreed to allow one Chinese to remain behind for each Chinese-owned store; the lone custodians could guarantee there would be no pilfering or destruction of Chinese stock. The rest, the entire Chinese community, assembled meekly and permitted themselves to be loaded, like so many cattle, into the horsedrawn drays and wagons. When the line of twenty-five vehicles was filled, the sad procession moved off – bumping, creaking, jostling in the springless wagons all the way to New Westminster where, under orders, the refugees boarded the steamer bound for Victoria. So the Chinese departed.

Victoria took almost immediate action against Vancouver. Indeed Victoria was delighted to vent its jealousy of Vancouver. In the aftermath of the anti-Chinese riots, the Assembly decided that Vancouver was incapable of governing itself and cancelled its city charter. It gathered a police force from among the unemployed in Victoria and dispatched them to administer Vancouver under the direction of Superintendent Raycroft. Van-couver felt deeply humiliated but, apart from a few rowdies who hurled scantling at the new police officers on their first day of duty, the town's citizens remained peaceable and co-operative.

Not even Victoria, however, could bring Locks-ley Lucas and the other riot leaders to justice. The police arrested two men, neither of them Locksley, and a special magistrate arrived from Victoria to try them. Both men were acquitted. "It was stated in court that the two ringleaders had gone to bed comparatively early," William Gallagher later wrote, "and it was said they had not left each other during the night, which was quite true. They had gone to bed comparatively early, got up again and gone to the riot, and then returned to the Sunnyside and gone to bed a second time."

Over the following few weeks many of Van-couver's permanent Chinese residents returned to their homes and shops in Chinatown. And on May 23, 1887, when the first transcontinental CPR train reached Vancouver – "the greatest event in the history of our city," Mayor Maclean declared– there were dozens of Chinese in the welcoming throng.

Edward Roper, an English author and artist, crossed Canada on the CPR in 1887. At New Westminster's boardwalk he sketched this scene of "the strange diversity of people who passed me by."

PRIDE OF THE TOBACCONIST

While cigarette smoking was slowly gaining in popularity, cigar, pipe and chewing tobacco manufacturers were continuing to satisfy the public appetite for the leaf. The earliest French settlers had adopted the old Indian practice, and year after year tobacco consumption increased. William Macdonald was well on his way to building a substantial empire on the business, and smaller firms in southwestern Ontario and Quebec's Montcalm, Joliette and Rouville counties were engaged in the delicate business of harvesting and curing the leaf. The well-to-do imported their own special blends from Cuba, then and still the source of the world's finest cigars. The decorative cigar box label (see page 21, the equestrienne and Lord Roberts labels at right and below) originated also in Cuba, but the popular home-grown brands like Old Flag, Invincible and Peg Top sent billows of smoke through gentlemen's clubs, billiard halls, drawing rooms and taverns in the country. Only the working classes indulged in chewing, and only notorious women "lit up."

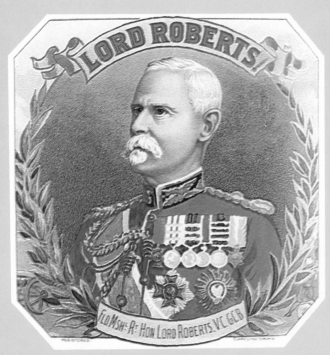

67

CHAPTER SIX

CAMPAIGN CLOWNS AND GOOD LONDON GIN

Whatever other faults Canadians may have, they are certainly willing... to serve...

Thomas Conant

A fervent, shouting, floor-shaking audience filled every seat, lined the walls and spilled over into the lobby of the Grand Opera House in London, Ontario, on the frozen, windy night of December 16, 1889. The feature attraction wasn't a touring opera company (the Boston Ideal Opera Company had drawn capacity crowds earlier in the year), not a minstrel show nor an orchestral display; it was not a musical event of any sort, though a small brass band was in attendance, recruited from the excellent local civic orchestra. The star of the evening was Mr. W. R. Meredith, Q.C., M.L.A., barrister, resident of London, friend to many listeners in the House, well-liked, a man, above all else, proud to single himself out among his contemporaries as that most distinctive citizen, a practising politician.

The show at the London Opera House was political, but not just *any* political rally. "The greatest demonstration in the political history, not only of London, but of the western counties of the Province of Ontario took place to-night," reported the Toronto *Empire*, "when Mr. W. R. Meredith delivered an address under the auspices of the Young Men's Liberal Conservative Association of London."

As a drawing card, Mr. Meredith did not at first seem especially powerful. True, he was the leader of the Conservative Opposition in the Ontario legislature and, true, a provincial election waited just a few months away. But Oliver Mowat's Liberals had banished Meredith into opposition for the seventeen years he'd sat in the legislature, and only a fool or a brilliantly optimistic Tory believed that Mowat would not do it again. Still, despite the gloomy prospects, the crowd flocked to the Opera House, radiating the special buoyant expectancy of an opening night audience. "Literally hundreds of citizens," said the *Empire,* "were unable to gain admittance to the hall or had to stand crushed against each other in the lobbies during the three hours the meeting occupied."

The House was decked out in Union Jacks, the gas jets flared dramatically, an inscription reading "God Save The Queen" hung over the platform and, as Mr. Meredith came on stage, the audience hailed him with vigorous applause. When he rose to speak a few minutes later, he received "a tremendous ovation." The band crashed into "For He's a Jolly Good Fellow", and the members of the audience who had arrived early enough to capture seats stood on them as the hall filled with clapping and whistling, with shouts of "hurrah" and cries of "hear, hear!" The ovation lasted a full five minutes and Chairman Bayly had to rap a dozen times for order.

Visitors who used these cards for admission to the galleries of the House of Commons in 1883 might have heard George Kirkpatrick, speaker of the House 1883-87, admonishing John A. and Opposition leader, Edward Blake, to abide by the rules of debate.

Opposite page: A cartoonist pokes fun at a politician's exaggerated concern for the welfare of his constituents–especially on the eve of an election.

**Oliver Mowat
Champion of "Our Country"**

When Oliver Mowat talked about "our country," he usually meant Ontario; when he spoke of himself, the term "Christian statesman" crept into his vocabulary. He was born in Kingston, U.C., in 1820, educated in law, and served briefly as a partner in John A. Macdonald's legal firm. In 1857 he entered politics, winning a seat in the Legislative Assembly of Canada. A "Father of Confederation," he retired from politics until 1872, when Edward Blake stepped down and the premier's mantle fell to Mowat. For a record twenty-four years, he served as head of the Liberal government in Ontario. He was a staunch Presbyterian, a man of high principles, and a strong defender of provincial rights–an area of the constitution in which he tussled with John A. on every available occasion.

An orator, Mr. Meredith was not. He leaned instead to a humble, dogged, occasionally unctuous delivery. "I cannot expect, sir," he began, "that a public man in the course of a career extending over seventeen or eighteen years, as mine has, will in all things have satisfied all of his constituents, but at all events I can say this: I have endeavoured at all times to discharge my duty as the chosen representative of the Conservative party, and according to my light as to what was for the best interests of this province and this country." His speech rolled on for two hours and thirty-five minutes, studded with lists of statistics, with lengthy quotes from correspondence and court records. And he forced his relentless way through an ample sampling of the day's burning issues: the tyranny of Mowat's liquor licence system, Grit finagling with timber resources, the heinous patronage practices of the provincial cabinet, and the evils of separate schools.

fire and enthusiasm

The audience loved it all. They devoured every revelation, statistic, quote, accusation and homily with rapt concentration, and at the appropriate intervals, they responded with applause and cries of "hear, hear." When Mr. Meredith at last stepped back with a final oratorical flourish, "Under all circumstances, I have had before me but one beacon light, the good of my country and of my Fatherland," the band and crowd whooped once again into "Jolly Good Fellow." Chairman Bayly moved that the gathering "pledge Mr. Meredith its confidence and support." The motion carried unanimously with a thunder of "ayes." Then an ultimate burst of applause as W. R. Meredith, Q.C., M.L.A. left the patform, and the crowd tumbled into the cold night, exhilarated, cheered, full of fire and enthusiasm for the world and loaded with enough fuel to carry them through

their political discussions until the next rally- maybe a week away, not more.

For all Canadians in a time when diversions were comparatively few and expensive, politics filled the multi-roles of sport, hobby, passion, conversation piece and action generator. It was one interest that involved citizens in the world beyond their village or farm or city block, and they pursued politics with zest. Rallies, parades, banquets, epic speechifying, head-to-head debates, pamphleteering – all activities that bore on politics flourished.

political show business

Political picnics blossomed as a pleasantly effective campaign device. The Tories had used them extensively in the summers preceding the federal election of 1878, with the aim of wooing rural voters. At these gatherings the whole countryside came together for Tory-sponsored open-air meals, beer and neighbourly talk. Sir John A. Macdonald proved himself all over again a masterly campaigner, and in the eighties the Conservatives made picnics a key element in all their politicking. The events tended to grow more sophisticated with the years, and the simple socializing began to approach show business. When Macdonald arrived at an affair near Kingston in September 1888, dressed to kill in his "tall white hat, black coat, red tie and light pantaloons," he had first to sit through "the gymnastic feats of the athletic Judge family and a troupe of fencers from Vienna in tights and short skirts" before he could make his way through the gathering with his "quips and cranks . . . nods and becks and wreathed smiles," which was for him the real purpose of the day.

These affairs – the picnics, the rallies, the banquets – were not always occasions for harmonious celebrations. Hand in hand with the happy devotion to politics went rugged partisanship. To a Tory, a Grit was the enemy – "a most *violent* Grit," Mackenzie Bowell habitually called every opposition member – and to a Grit, a Tory was a man just naturally worthy of scorn. "The Liberals have adopted the plan now of breaking down the personal character of every man who happens to be opposed to them," Macdonald's minister of the interior, Thomas White, told a wisely nodding audience at Mono Mills, Ontario, on June 10, 1886. "I have been told that this policy was agreed upon in caucus, Mr. Blake [the leader] being present at the caucus, and that each man was apportioned his part of this dirty work of slander."

This sort of partisanship turned many political meetings into raucous events, vehicles as much for hecklers and catcallers in the audience as for the advertised speakers. Frequently meetings descended into violence. In some cases the rough stuff was just a matter of overcrowding – or overzealousness. More often, the violence wasn't so incidental – it was downright calculated. Especially in Ontario, where Tory Orangemen could be counted on to stir up hot passions, men sometimes carried clubs and other mildly lethal weapons to political gatherings to defend their party allegiance. Bloodshed, or at least a severe knock or two, often followed.

inter-party rancour

A correspondent for the *Evening Telegram* witnessed one typically rowdy rally at Stannes Hall in Ottawa in June 1882. "The several speakers were frequently obliged to resume their seats until the side fights were settled. Three prominent and obstreperous individuals were thrown out, one having his head badly bruised, and the other two had their heads fractured. Another meeting is called for this evening in the Canadian Institute when there is sure to be a disturbance. A posse of police will be in attendance."

'ALE FELLOW, WELL MET!

"HE TRUSTED THAT THE BUSINESS WOULD SO CONTINUE TO INCREASE THAT THE PROPRIETORS WOULD FIND THEMSELVES CRAMPED FOR ROOM, AND BE OBLIGED, IN CONSEQUENCE, TO EXTEND THEIR QUARTERS."

Politics and private morality collided when New Brunswick's teetotaling Leonard Tilley was asked to congratulate the Dartmouth Brewery as a model of prosperity under the Tories.

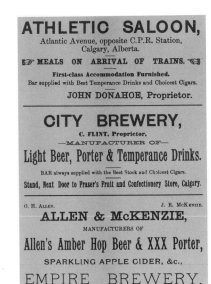

A tippling Scot and friends at a bar in High River, Alta. (formerly Camp Spitzie). Note the spittoons and tobacco-stained floor.

The inter-party rancour affected life at almost every level. Manufacturers pressured employees to vote their way, which happened to be Tory; husbands and fathers directed older sons to their political allegiances (their wives lacked a vote); and Orange lodges set out to intimidate everyone with a ballot to cast. Even social contacts were formed along strict party lines. In this, the country's hostesses took their lead from Ottawa. A writer for the *Week* pointed out in the issue of April 10, 1884:

In the days of Reform rule the wife of the prime minister entertained the Tories as well as the Grits, and other ladies followed her example. Now there are few houses in which members of the opposite factions still meet under the same roof, and at dinner at Rideau Hall, and at those given by the Speaker of each branch of the Legislature the wolf lies down with the lamb. But, as a rule, the cleavage of politics regulates the social cleavage.

But, it was in man-to-man contests between two candidates for office that political bitterness emerged most venomously. The name-calling was frank, acid and frequently hilarious. But accusations and insults made up only a small, if noisy, part of a politician's repertoire. He had also to equip himself and his cronies with a variety of even more aggressive tactics, most of them nasty, if he hoped to out-manoeuvre the opposition. One favourite device available only to an incumbent M.P. was to gear the official riding machinery to hinder and harass the opposition candidate. In the riding of East Toronto, just before the federal election of 1882, a Grit named James Beaty presented himself to the returning officer, Alderman Blevins, with his nomination papers in hand. The alderman, an old Tory, rejected Beaty's nomination because, he said, some of the names on the papers were illegible. Beaty promptly gathered new and legible names on a second batch of papers. Blevins again refused him, this time on the improbable grounds

72

The St. Charles Hotel tap room was a place where Victoria's entrepreneurs and politicians could quaff a pint of stout.

that Beaty's nomination fee of $200 was tendered in Dominion bank notes and not in gold. "This is the way I have been humbugged out of my nomination," Beaty announced to the press. "But it is not finished yet. I will upset the election in East Toronto. My solicitors will see to that."

Attacking an election result in court was a widely employed tactic in the eighties. The 1870s Liberal government of Alexander Mackenzie had obligingly passed the Controverted Elections Act, a statute so strict that clever lawyers, acting on behalf of defeated candidates, regularly used it to void elections. Even if the "grounds" were totally spurious, it often seemed good strategy for election losers to challenge the winner simply to make the opposition spend money. It was especially useful for Tories, whose coffers were always overflowing, to attack Grits, whose bank accounts were usually overdrawn.

Tory money was also used in the sinister business of importing votes. At every election,

Conservative organizers in ridings close to the American border made lists of Canadians who had moved to nearby American cities but who, mysteriously, still appeared on local voting lists. Then the Tories treated the expatriates to a free trip back home – in return for their votes. Sir Richard Cartwright, a Liberal front-bencher, was convinced that these voters contributed to the victorious Tory margins in many close elections. "I should say that the foreign vote, as it was generally called, averaged from one hundred to two hundred in most closely contested ridings, and sometimes much more," he related in his *Reminiscences*. "In fact one of Sir John's own colleagues openly boasted to me that they could, if need be, bring in 20,000 outside voters to counteract what he was pleased to call 'my devilish machinations.'"

For the Grits, an even more villainous Tory trick was the massive gerrymander of 1882. Macdonald claimed he was merely "equalizing the population" to ensure "representation by popula-

ELECTION TIME

Election time in the eighties was still a business of privilege. Women, of course, were not allowed to vote and exerted their influence through propertied husbands. In 1885, the Tories rammed through national voter qualifications against a bitter opposition, but a controversial clause extending the franchise to some women was withdrawn before passage. The secret ballot, adopted first by New Brunswick in 1855, had come into use in all the provinces (except P.E.I.) in the '70s, but details of civic elections were left to the sometimes dubious discretion of town and city councils.

Henri Julien's poor confused voter–enticed in the late 1880s by the Liberals' "pie in the sky" platform of commercial union with the U.S.

FACTS FOR THE ELECTORS !

Incorporation as a City a Delusion and a Snare !

It will raise your Taxes 3 Mills or $3 on every Thousand of your Assessment.

We now pay the County for all purposes, $1,385 00	
We get back from the County for roads and bridges,	203.72
Constable's fees,	401.90
Grant for High School,	1457.13
	2062.75

Balance in our favor, $677.75

If we become a City—

A board of Police Commissioners will cost us at least	$1000.00
The use of the County building and criminal justice,	2500.00
Increase in Police Magistrate's salary,	400.00
Grant to the High School,	1457.13
Beside, we shall have to build and maintain a Lock Up.	

Balance against us under Incorporation, $5,357.13

On our assessment of $2,083,690 this means very nearly **3 Mills** on the Dollar **or *$3.00 increase on every $1,000.00* of our assessment.**

Vote against the Gentlemen who are asking every elector to say yea, or nay, next Monday, which is illegal, and against good government, *which is by ballot.* Mayor Francis says it is for the purpose of saving *Two whole dollars,* the cost of Ballot papers. Don't you forget it !

FRANCIS, WILSON & CO. are seeking to Disfranchise 300 working men by means of Incorporation as a City. **Vote against such men.**

The qualification for votes by incorporation will be raised 33⅓ per cent., from $300 to $400. See Revised Statutes Ont. for 1883, P 13 5.

Qualification for Councillors, Reeves and Mayor in Cities on leasehold is $2000. See Ont. Revised Statutes for 1887, Chap. 29. Section 73. For towns $1200 only.

Vote against the Measure and the Men Likewise, who would prevent the Laboring Men and Mechanics from seeking a seat at the Council Board.

Remember a **Lower Rate of Taxation** can only be obtained at present by an **Increase in the Assessment;** or in other words by *Cutting off your Nose to Spite Your Face.*

The histories of young cities, such as St. Thomas, Stratford, Brantford, St. Catherines, and Belleville are **Caution Signals Against Incorporation.**

We are now a prosperous, progressive town Let us keep so until we can claim a right to become a city, which will be time enough. The Statutory number of inhabitants is **15,000.** At present we would look like a Baby-in-Long-Clothes-City. **Vote it Down.**

JOSEPH RIPPON, Candidate for St. George's Ward.

The cost of a town becoming a city–a common election issue in a rapidly urbanizing nation. Handbills stacked statistics against the incumbent mayor.

tion." But the extraordinarily complicated mano-euvres he set in motion to achieve his aim suggest-ed he had funnier business in mind. In Ontario alone, in order to add just four new seats to the province's representation in the Commons, he shifted the boundaries in fifty-four ridings. The Liberals contended that he had sliced up these ridings in such a crafty way that marginal Con-servative ridings received more Tory votes from adjacent safer ridings and he had isolated ridings that voted Liberal anyway. Although historians are still arguing about the gerrymander's effects, the voting statistics seemed to support the Liberal charges. In the elections of '82 and '87, the Tories showed slim popular majorities in Ontario of 2,439 and 3,156 votes respectively, and in the 1891 elections, the Grits actually out-polled the Tories in the province by 3,947 votes; yet in all three elections, the Conservatives came out with parlia-mentary majorities of from fourteen to eighteen seats. "The gerrymander act," Sir Richard Cart-wright commented sadly, "was a mean and cow-ardly trick."

brewers and distillers

Sir Richard and his Liberal friends grew almost as exercised over the Tories' cozy relation-ship with the rich and powerful Canadian liquor industry. The Conservatives were traditionally the boozers among Canadian politicians, the Grits were the teetotaling champions of temperance. The entire Tory cabinet, when presented at the Mar-quis of Lorne's first state dinner in 1879, became so helplessly drunk that they "caused scandal," in the words of the Ottawa *Citizen*, "by their uproari-ous behaviour." The Tories didn't mind the criti-cism. For them, liquor meant money since the Gooderhams, the Carlings, the O'Keefes and the other liquor and beer dynasties of Canada were good Conservatives, (in fact John Carling was

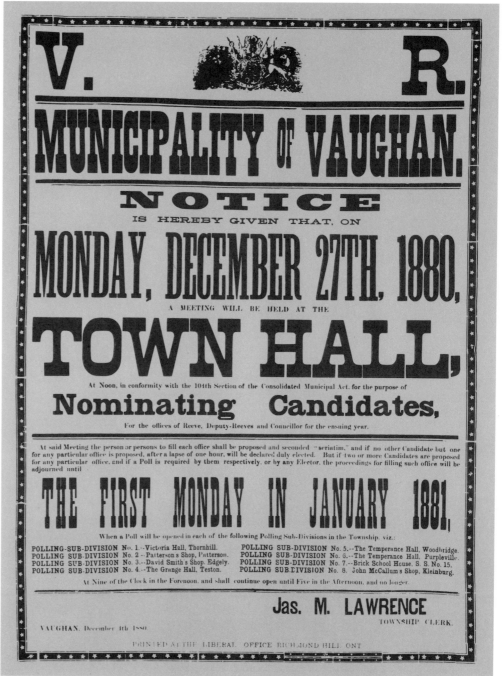

Meetings for nominating candidates for municipal office preceded the first-Monday-in-January election day. If a single candidate stood unopposed for one hour, he was declared "duly elected."

75

John Carling
Brewer and Politician

If anyone knew about the politics of prohibition, John Carling did. Born in 1828, in London, U. C., he grew up in the shadow of his father's City Brewery, joined the family business, and began his long political career in 1857. The gloomy camp of Ontario's prohibitionist Liberals was no place for a man whose business depended on ale flowing freely to the province's 5–6,000 taverns. He fell in with the Conservatives, held several cabinet posts in Macdonald's government, and gave considerable support to the Tory cause and coffers. He was one of the chief opponents of the 1875 tavern licence (Crooks) Act of Ontario, and the architect of pro-liquor legislation amendments by the Tories. Minister of agriculture from 1885–92, he set up the Dominion Experimental Farms.

minister of agriculture). At election time they could be counted on to pour generous sums of money into Tory campaign treasuries.

For the voting public, liquor meant turmoil. In almost every county, in elections at every level– Dominion, provincial, municipal – the characters and social inclinations of the candidates turned the contests into rowdy confrontations over temperance issues. The Scott Act, passed by the Liberals in 1878, turned out to be political suicide for the Grits. "At the time there were five or six thousand hotel and tavern keepers in Ontario alone," Sir Richard Cartwright recalled, "and each of them personally controlled quite a number of votes."

drys versus wets

In a pattern that was repeated in many counties, Bruce County in Ontario called on its citizens to make a decision on the liquor question seven times in the years from 1878 to 1902. The hottest, most bitter vote occurred in 1884. "The campaign commenced early in the year with the obtaining of the signatures of 3,790 ratepayers to a requisition praying that the Act be submitted to the electors to be voted on," wrote Norman Robertson, Bruce County treasurer. "During the summer, public meetings were held in many localities to discuss the features of the Act. Speakers from outside places were obtained by both parties to stump the county. Literature was freely circulated, and every means used to enlighten the electors." Finally, on October 30 the voters cast their ballots, and the drys won by 1,321 votes. But less than four years later, the county endured another campaign, just as bitterly contested, and this time the wets won by 1,392 votes, a victory that lasted only until 1894 when, alas, the drys won again.

Still, despite the exhausting arguments over questions like the liquor issue, despite the general name-calling, bad-tempered debating and nasty manoeuvering, despite all the perils of politics, there was never any shortage of candidates for political office in Canada. "Whatever other faults Canadians may have," wrote Thomas Conant, a social historian of the eighties, "they are certainly willing, with all possible alacrity, to serve their countrymen in the way of filling offices, small or important, throughout the country." Some candidates were motivated by the opportunity for personal gain, the opportunity to hand out patronage; some found the pay, slender as it was, a strong attraction (federal M.P.s received $1,000 per year; Ontario M.L.A.s $400); some simply wanted to serve. But all of them, no matter what other motive impelled them, were drawn by one happy circumstance of late nineteenth-century Canadian life – the fame and celebrity and recognition that naturally accompanied every political office.

a different breed

Politicians were honoured, their praises sung. "Two miles of torches on a dark soft night," Macdonald wrote to Sir Charles Tupper in 1885 after an evening held in tribute to him in Montreal, "the air filled with fireworks wherever we went. The whole people of the city in the streets. The banquet a marvel of skill and decoration." Those were the days when politics occupied an important emotional part of every citizen's life, when politicians filled the roles that in the 20th century fell to show-business celebrities and athletes. Politics was one of society's games and politicians were society's heroes and villains, a different breed of man.

The eighties were quiet times for Victoria and the Retreat Saloon. With Vancouver as the CPR terminus, there was even talk of moving the capital to the mainland.

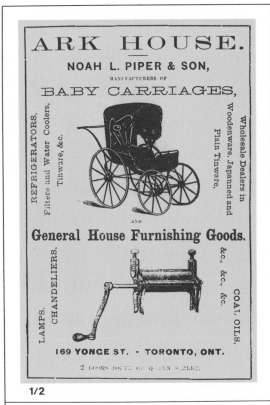

1/2

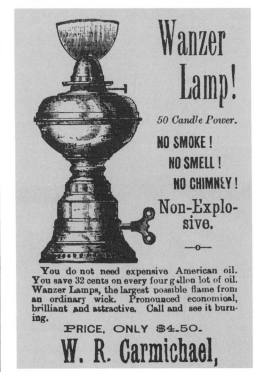

3

4

5

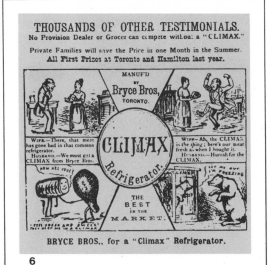

6

HOUSEHOLD CONVENIENCES

Everyday life may not have been easy for most people in the eighties, but it was getting better. Babies were wheeled around in wicker perambulators (1); Monday's wash was cranked through the corrugated wooden rollers of the "washing machine" (2) until it was clean; lighting was by kerosene or coal-oil lamp (3), though wealthier families boasted of gas lamps; guests of the well-to-do perched on the edges of horsehair or brocade-covered parlour chairs (4) talking of politics, fashion or weather; farmers' wives and children might churn the week's butter in a new Union box churn (5); some people even had "refrigerators" (6)—just a fancy name for an ice-box; fires were common, but Ball's Fire Escape (7) was at hand for the rescue; in the fashionable parts of town, houses had a self-flushing indoor cistern (8) or a dry earth closet (9)—rural folks still visited the good old "house of parliament" out in the back; young men in business typed their letters on a new-fangled machine, the typewriter (10); and the treadle sewing machine (11) had cut the work of housewives, tailors, seamstresses and dressmakers in half. There was even serious talk that some day soon electricity would run almost everything!

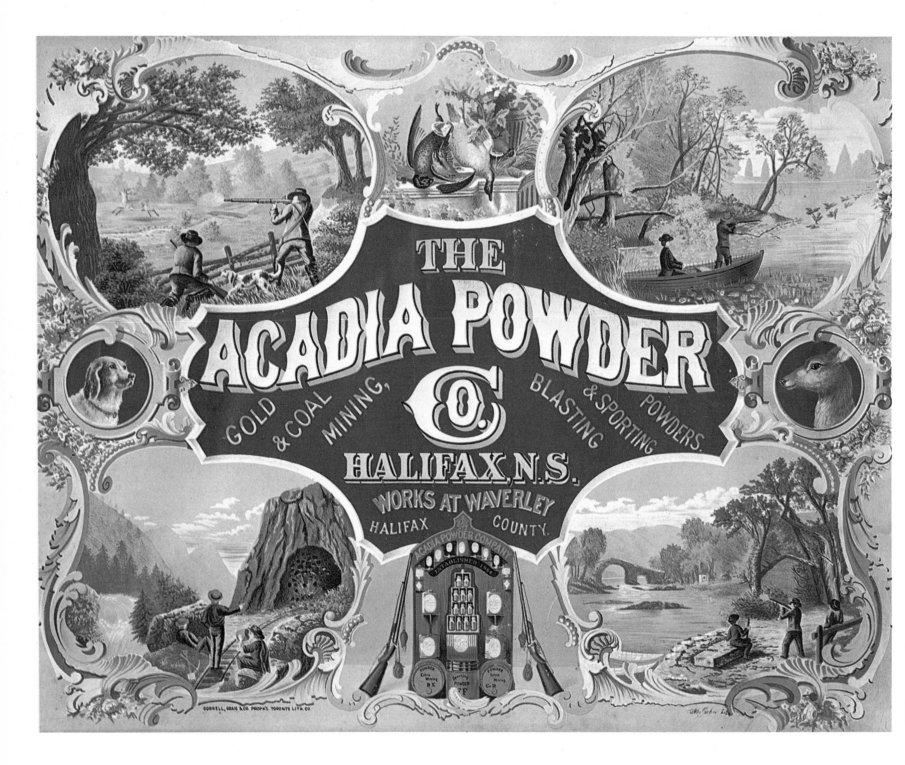

CHAPTER SEVEN

DRYDOCK DAYS AND MARITIME PRIDE

There are dreams go down the harbor
With the tall ships of St. John.

Bliss Carman, "The Ships of St. John"

The day the sleek clipper ship, *Orquell*, was launched, all the kids in Pictou, Nova Scotia, were let out of school early. It was a shiny, optimistic spring day, May 22, 1879, and in the bustling sailing town on the Northumberland Strait, hundreds of citizens were gathering on Battery Hill and the other hills that sloped down to the J. and J. Yorston shipyards in the harbour. People had flocked across the strait from Prince Edward Island; they'd come in from Pictou Island and Caribou Island, from the Merigomish shore to the east and from Toney River, Mount Thom, Dalhousie Mountain and Hardwood Hill to the west. They greeted and spoke to one another in broad north-of-Scotland accents. Pictou County was populated by some thirty thousand stout Highlanders, and for many of them Gaelic was an easier language to handle than English.

Precisely at noon, marked by the tinny chime of the ancient town hall clock, the crowd held quiet and a dozen yard hands began walloping the chocks that held the *Orquell* in place. The ship swooped gracefully down the ramp, plunged under water almost to her deck line and then, heaving off a dense, swishing spray, slipped across the still

harbour with overpowering majesty. The crowds let out a thunderous cheer that bounced and echoed off the hills; the school children waved their flags – Union Jacks and Yorston house flags, and when everyone grew still, Captain William Joe Foster, the *Orquell*'s first and, as it turned out, only master, spoke briefly and modestly, and everyone cheered again. It was a regatta day, a holiday, a celebration day, all good times rolled into one and, after the ceremony, kids and adults headed back up Battery Hill to the town hall for the grand luncheon prepared by Pictou's ladies.

Perhaps the fate of the *Orquell*, the pride of the Pictou fleet, symbolized the predicament of the Maritimes in the 1880s. At first the *Orquell* sailed with all the speed and energy predicted by her builders and owners, the Yorstons. In one remarkable run she sailed from Pictou harbour to Lundy Island just off the west coast of England in a breath-taking eleven days, the fastest time recorded by a clipper ship up to the mid-eighties. But the *Orquell* was forced to subject herself and her crew to an unending strain in order to compete with the mighty iron and steam ships, in order to turn a small profit for her owners.

Early in September 1887, driving out of Barrow-In-Furness, England, with a heavy cargo of iron ore, the *Orquell* ran head on into a wild ripping gale. Normally Captain William Joe Foster would have turned back to port, but the

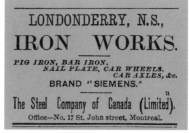

By the 1880s, the days of the great soft-wood windships were numbered, and iron-plate vessels were taking over the trans-Atlantic trade. More and more industries were looking to ore- and coal-rich regions of Nova Scotia for resources, and by 1883, the date of this ad, steel companies had already located in the province.

Opposite page: The sporting life in Nova Scotia–a hunter's paradise portrayed in a hand-painted display sign for the Acadia Powder Company.

The H.M.S. Canada in drydock at Halifax—one of the last (and largest) Maritime-built ships to *sail the Atlantic and West Indian trade routes that had once been the mainstay of the economy.*

Orquell couldn't afford a lost day, not when there were steam ships on the seas to worry about. For twenty-four hours the ship held up to the storm's battering. The wind tore the sails, smashed the lifeboats, shook the hull. And at last the *Orquell* was beaten. A ship came by, a steamer, and took off Captain Foster and his crew. On September 6, 1887, the *Orquell* sank to the bottom of the English Channel; in Pictou flags flew at half mast.

The Maritimers' secret was simple – they loved the sea and they loved the sailing ships that assured them of their place in the world's business. In the middle decades of the century, Sunday crowds strolled along Water Street in Halifax just to revel in the forest of masts on the ships pulled in for loading at the sheds that ran the length of the street. In Saint John, New Brunswick, kids headed straight from school to the docks at the foot of Princess Street where they soaked up the magic of the spar-makers, the riggers, the stevedores and sail-makers and, most of all, of the sailors who had shipped out from Saint John, then returned home from exotic foreign ports. A favourite Maritimer's anecdote concerned Rufus Choate, a great Nova Scotia businessman. When on his deathbed in his house on Halifax harbour, he instructed his doctors and family, "If a schooner or sloop goes by, don't disturb me. But if there is a square-rigged ship, wake me up."

declining usefulness

In the eighties the Maritimes discovered that a love of ships and a passion for the sea weren't enough. Something more prosaic and tougher than mere emotion – iron combined with steam – came along to rob the three provinces of their sailing-ship security. Ships driven by steam, not wind, and built of iron, not wood, proved not only more reliable but roomier and more economical to operate. By the eighties, Maritime sailing ships were entering a period of declining usefulness.

Ship-building fell off sharply. Prince Edward Island's yards had turned out 914 clippers and barques between 1861 and 1870, but in the eighties they built a mere 132 ships of all sizes. Yarmouth, once the thriving centre of Nova Scotia's ship-building industry, accounted for only six new vessels in 1880, five in 1882, four in 1884 and in 1887 it added not one deep-sea sailing ship to its fleet, the first blank year in a century. The last large ship built in New Brunswick was the *John McLeod*, weighing 1,600 tons, launched in 1885 by Captain John McLeod, M.L.A., at Black River near Saint John. In Saint John itself, only 2,000 men made their living in ship-construction and all its allied trades by 1888. The city fathers held worried meetings to discuss the unemployment crisis.

look to the land

Everything conspired against wooden ships. Lloyd's and the other insurers preferred iron vessels and steadily raised their rates on Maritime clippers. When a wooden ship's insurance classification period, usually ten or twelve years, ran out, the insurers demanded extensive repairs before they'd reclassify it. The owners invariably lacked the money to finance an overhauling and chose instead to sell off their ships. By the end of the eighties, there were more Maritimes-built ships sailing under the Norwegian flag than under any other flag, including Canada's.

Many of the younger Maritime sailors followed the ships out of the country. Many more turned to steam ships and signed on with the W.R. Grace Company, the United Fruit Company and a few other British and American lines. Older sailors, apart from the Bluenose mates who were always in demand, suffered more from the dwindling Maritime fleet. They were forced to abandon the sea and look to the land, to become, reluctantly, farmers.

The eighties were not a time of prosperity and expansion for any province of the Maritimes. Between the census of 1881 and the census of 1891, the population of New Brunswick increased by exactly thirty people. Nova Scotia's population rose in the same period by slightly under ten thousand souls and Prince Edward Island's by 187.

a contemplative quality

Economic hardship inclined Maritimers to withdraw socially and culturally into their own ways of living and to ignore the rest of Canada. They were given to frequent grumbling over the bad deal they had received in Confederation from Upper Canadians who still refused to buy Maritimes lumber and coal; the custom of flying flags at half mast on July 1 hung on in many Atlantic communities.

But Maritime cities were not culturally deprived. The people of Saint John, New Brunswick, regularly filled the Mechanics' Institute on Germain Street on lecture nights, and every kind of musical and dramatic entertainment attracted cheering crowds to their 2,000-seat Academy of Music. Further up-river, in Fredericton, social and cultural life had a more contemplative quality. Fredericton was, to its immense pride, a university town. The University of New Brunswick and its professors exercised as much influence on the city's style of life as its businessmen and politicians did. "There was in Fredericton," George Parkin, a teacher of English literature later recalled, "an old-fashioned courtesy and dignity – a real interest in things of the mind and spirit." The gentle atmosphere of Fredericton nurtured in those years the first distinctive literary community in Canada, centred around the poetry and personalities of Charles G.D. Roberts and his cousin Bliss Car-

The Intercolonial's claims of speed, comfort and safety were quite true: express trains took just over fifty hours to travel the route from Halifax to Toronto in 1882, a mere half-a-day more than it takes for the trip today. Critics, however, contended that the publicly owned line was one of the worst-managed in North America.

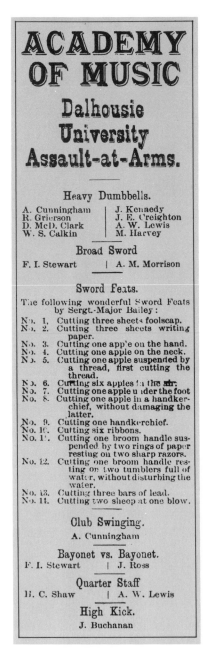

This "assault-at-arms" featured such shows of skill as club swinging, stick drill, a boxing mêlée and incredible sword feats by Sgt.-Maj. Bailey.

Chamber music concerts of the Halifax Haydn Club were highlights of the cultural season for the city's "drawing-room society."

man, graduates of University of New Brunswick.

Neither of New Brunswick's two principal cities offered much beauty to the eye. The cities occupied a secondary position to the countryside, since New Brunswick was a fragmented world, each river valley nurturing its own isolated community life. Each was based principally in agriculture and was as honest and sturdy as the names of the villages that dotted the province: Watt, Whitney and Welsford, Doaktown, Tweedside, Durham and Head of Mill Stream, Blackville, Upper Blackville, Peterville, Gunningsville and Blissville. The names were, of course, distinctly Anglo-Saxon; of New Brunswick's 321,233 citizens recorded in the 1881 census, fully 244,499 were of Scots, Irish or English origin.

Saint John, for its part, was enduring a difficult period. The terrible fire of 1877 had wiped out two thirds of the city, razed 1,660 houses, left 13,000 men, women and children homeless, and run up a property loss calculated at $27,000,000. Saint John rallied from the devastation, and by the early 1880s it could boast of its forty-one churches (most notably Trinity Church, an elegant, grey, stone edifice with a huge clock by whose chimes every citizen marked his day's progress), four banks, four daily newspapers (three of them Tory and one, the lively *Sun*, Grit) and of the really splendid fountain that stood in Market Square.

Even if Saint John had tumbled from its rank as the world's fourth busiest sea port, its citizens showed admirable verve. On almost every summer weekend, one of the local fraternal organizations planned a moonlight excursion on the St. John River, an occasion invariably enlivened by the skilful melodies of Harrison's Orchestra. In May 1885, an enterprising promoter brought John L. Sullivan to town. About two thousand men flocked

Opera house audiences thrilled to the wit and music of Gilbert & Sullivan. This is the 1885 Halifax cast of Pirates of Penzance.

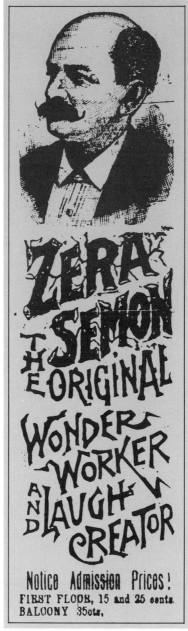

Vaudeville was in its heyday, and the Lyceum Theatre in Halifax was packed to the rafters by touring minstrel and novelty companies like Zera Semon's.

to the Victoria Skating Rink to see the great man box a few rounds with four different opponents. More solemnly, in the very week that Sullivan appeared in town, Saint John's citizens gathered at the ferry landing at the foot of Princess Street to see off the local men of the 62nd Battalion who were ordered west to fight Riel. " 'Goodbye, Sweetheart, Goodbye' by the City Concert Band touched a sympathetic chord in the hearts of many," reported the *Sun*, "and they strove hard to repress the tears which came unbidden."

Saint John's influence on the Maritimes extended scarcely beyond its own city limits. But Halifax was different – it reigned undeniably as the dominant centre of Nova Scotia, if not of the entire Maritimes.

It boasted, to begin with, an active cultural life. Halifax opened its Victoria School of Art and Design in 1887 and installed as first head master

Nova Scotia's best-known painter, a landscape specialist named George Harvey. The ladies of Halifax's best families competed among each other for the chance to take art lessons from Matilda Maude Crane at her quaint studios on Morris Street. What principally attracted the ladies was Miss Crane's unique specialty – she was the first artist in Canada to teach china painting. The city considered its new bandstand something unique, too; completed in the Public Gardens in the summer of 1887, it was an out-sized, ornate structure, just right for the brilliantly attired military bands that held forth in concert every Thursday evening.

But, most of all, theatre flourished in Halifax in those years. The city had opened its Academy of Music on January 9, 1877, a handsome brick and stucco edifice on Barrington Street with a frescoed ceiling and the biggest chandelier in Nova Scotia.

A YOUNG MARITIME POET

Bliss Carman

Sitting toward the back of his class
at the University of New Brunswick
in 1881 (a college of forty students
and four professors), Bliss Carman
was grappling with the obscurities
of the classics. His cousin, Charles
G.D. Roberts, graduated two years
before, was already making his mark
as a poet, and Carman, born in 1861
in Fredericton, had chosen the poet's
life for himself. But recognition was
slow in coming. After his father's
death in 1885, he left Canada and
worked at journalism to pay the rent,
all the while continuing to write.
His first volume, *Low Tide on Grand
Pré* (1893), represents the best of his
early work, and many of his later
volumes of verse recall his boyhood.
Regarded as one of the major poets
of the post-Confederation period,
Carman never returned to live in
Canada, and most of his twenty-six
books first appeared in the U.S.

A Windflower

Between the roadside and the wood,
Between the dawning and the dew,
A tiny flower before the sun,
Ephemeral in time, I grew.

And there upon the trail of spring,
Not death nor love nor any name
Known among men in all their lands
Could blur the wild desire with shame.

But down my dayspan of the year
The feet of straying winds came by;
And all my trembling soul was thrilled
To follow one lost mountain cry.

And then my heart beat once and broke
To hear the sweeping rain forebode
Some ruin in the April world,
Between the woodside and the road.

To-night can bring no healing now;
The calm of yesternight is gone;
Surely the wind is but the wind,
And I a broken waif thereon.

In the early 1880s, the most fashionable activity in town was attending the Academy for theatricals by touring American groups – "Camilla's Husband" and "Uncle Tom's Cabin" were the sure-fire draws of the 1883 season; for concerts by the Halifax Symphony Orchestra under conductor Max Weil, a European import; and for operettas presented by local amateurs from the St. Mary's Dramatic Club, the St. Patrick's Ministrels and the musically inclined sailors of H.M.S. *Bellerophon, Northampton* and *Emerald*, all ships on permanent guard duty in Halifax harbour.

musicians and magicians

The enterprising members of the Young Men's Literary Association took over Halifax's old Temperance Hall in 1880, slapped on a few bright coats of red and yellow paint, renamed the place the Lyceum and proceeded to stage high-toned programmes of dramatic, literary and musical entertainments. The shows in the smaller upstairs theatre in the Lyceum weren't quite so uplifting. The upstairs was devoted to minstrel shows and, most of all, to the curious give-away shows masterminded by a touring magician named Zera Semon. Besides offering audiences displays of his own formidable legerdemain and of the musical skills of H. Price Webber's Boston Comedy Company, Semon used to hand out free prizes, and *that* drew huge turn-away crowds every time. In one remarkable two weeks in 1883, he distributed among his grateful audiences over $1,500 worth of presents– gifts ranging from gold-filled watches to corn brooms. It was the talk, or the scandal, of Halifax.

To many proper Haligonians, some of the touring lecturers who visited the city were almost as suspect as Zera Semon. William Jennings Bryan, Henry Ward Beecher and the Salvation Army's General Booth, all of whom spoke to full houses at the Academy in 1882, were of course perfectly respectable. But Oscar Wilde, who also appeared in 1882, seemed a more dubious case. The *Presbyterian Witness* objected to the presence in Halifax of "the conceited idiot Oscar Wilde" on the plain grounds that "a man who has written as Oscar has is not a desirable associate in any decent society." The *Witness* was, in the end, a minority voice. "A large number of the best people of Halifax had their curiosity satisfied last night by the sight of the celebrated aesthete," reported the *Acadian Recorder*, "for never since the opening of the Academy of Music was such an audience gathered together, at the same time so large and so fashionable."

All roads led to Halifax. It was the eastern terminus of the Intercolonial Railway, and it was the indispensable market for the fruits and vegetables of the Annapolis Valley and for the coal of Pictou's "Black Country of the Dominion." It claimed international prestige, too, as one of the four posts of "the marine quadrilateral of England." Malta, Gibraltar, Bermuda and Halifax–Britain kept each permanently armed as a defence against attack from any quarter, specifically in the 1880s against attack from Bismarck's Germany.

a garrison town

Halifax was thus Canada's last garrison town, and, to the residents, that status was both a blessing and a curse. Merchants welcomed the spending power of the two Imperial regiments stationed in the city and of the crews from the warships that regularly put in to Halifax's harbour. Military building contracts kept many Haligonians employed; in 1885 the British began construction of a formidable new fort on the old Peter McNab estate at a cost of $24,000 and in 1889 they ordered a new drydock built just north of the Halifax Dockyard for the use of the Royal Navy. Besides, the cheerful scarlet and gold uniforms of the military lent a special dash to Halifax's streets and the parties in the grand mansions of south-end Halifax could hardly have functioned without the presence of the handsome young Imperial officers.

the Hollis Street affair

Not everyone celebrated the presence of the British troops. The *Acadian Recorder* insisted in an editorial that those handsome young officers were actually "drones living on the labour of others" who displayed "the luxury of 'having nothing to do' in such attractive colours that the minds of our youth become so warped that they cannot appreciate the dignity of labour." Many citizens objected to the large acreage of land owned by the Imperial government, tax free, in the centre of town and along half the length of the waterfront. And they blamed the visiting soldiers and sailors for keeping in business the ladies of the night who prowled the saloons along Water Street. Indeed, the citizens often blamed the British for keeping the saloons themselves in operation.

Occasionally the quiet animosity between troops and civilians broke into open scandal. One Friday evening, August 27, 1880, two soldiers from the 97th Regiment with a little too much Water Street rum in their bellies set out on a rampage up Hollis Street. The two tommies took off their belts, swung the buckles over their heads and proceeded to smash the plate glass windows in two brokerage firms, Freeman Elliott's Men's Furnishing Shop, Ross the jeweller's and Godkin the merchant tailor's. When the two reached Eager's Drug Store, Mr. Eager himself sallied out to defend his property and held the soldiers off long enough for a policeman to arrive and haul them into custody, though not before they had racked up $1,500 worth of destruction.

"The outrage is one of the most villainous to

George Harvey
Teacher of Art and Design

While the Toronto and Montreal art world was aflurry with activity in the early eighties, formal education in fine art in Maritime Canada was still a fledgling enterprise. In 1881, however, when the Royal Canadian Academy held its first exhibition in Halifax, the establishment of an art school became the *cause célèbre* for George Harvey, an English landscape painter recently arrived in Halifax. In 1887, with cooperation from local private academies, he mounted an art exhibition of gigantic proportions containing everything from paintings and engravings to bric-a-brac and letters from the King of Siam. The exhibit, however questionable its artistic merit, served its fund-raising purpose in establishing the Victoria School of Art and Design, forerunner of today's Nova Scotia College of Art.

Tennis or riding, anyone? These gents from Halifax are dressed to take on all challengers. Tennis was played with a hard rubber ball and rackets shaped like those above. The "sports clothes" are the latest style, and the moustache adds a manly accent.

occur in Halifax for a long time," the *Morning Herald* fumed next day. "Who is to pay for it? We think the military should, for they are to blame for allowing such desperadoes to go out at large on our streets." The *Herald* declared itself satisfied, and so did the merchants of Hollis Street, when Nova Scotia's Chief Justice Sir William Young convicted the two soldiers of malicious injury and sentenced each to the penitentiary for eight years.

In its more typical, calmer moments, Halifax was a charming, generous, hospitable city. True, the salt water tended to invest its buildings with a dingy grey look. But Halifax offered other attractions that made it a regular stopping point for American tourists, 2,000 of them in the summer of 1882 alone. The city was certainly up to date; by 1886 it had replaced all but 200 of its gas lamps with the latest in electric lights, and by 1888 there were 400 telephones in the city. Halifax's young men devoted themselves to baseball at the Garrison Cricket Ground and hockey at the Dartmouth Rink where teams from Dalhousie College, the Royal Blue Athletic Club, the Victoria Club of Dartmouth and the Wanderers' Amateur Athletic Association competed.

The Wanderers, a group of the city's most spirited young bloods, got together in 1882 and immediately proved themselves so proficient and victorious in cricket, football, hockey and track that the whole city rallied behind them. City Council granted them a long lease at a nominal rental to a choice piece of land on Sackville Street opposite the Public Gardens. In 1888 they finished converting the property into the grandest playing fields in the entire Maritimes and from that year on, sporting Haligonians made the Wanderers' fields the city's centre for athletic events of every variety.

Every special occasion – Queen Victoria's birthday, the city's own birthday (known locally as Natal Day, "the day the British came over"), and Dominion Day – was celebrated with regattas in the harbour, tournaments at the South End Lawn Tennis Courts, half a dozen contests at the Wanderers' fields, float parades, parties and, generally, an atmosphere of universal joy.

Of all celebrations in the 1880s, probably the most memorable, not the least for its nostalgic quality, was the carnival on June 21, 1889, that marked Halifax's 140th birthday. The celebration began with a magnificent parade of decorated floats, army and navy bands and swinging marchers from the local fire department, the trade unions and the athletic clubs. Once the parade was over, the athletes headed for the Common, where they competed in a track meet to the cheers of a huge standing crowd. Later in the afternoon, competitors and audience moved to the harbour for another series of contests, this time in canoes and racing shells.

The climactic event of the day was a mock battle between the British ships anchored in the harbour and the British troops stationed in the Citadel, the military garrison on the hill high above the harbour. Navy and army executed their manoeuvres with all proper tactical skill. Both sides thundered away and the "battle" offered all the thrills of authentic combat. It was exciting stuff, but for many Haligonians it was also a slightly wistful occasion. After all, the ships in the harbour that day were British ships and, more than that, they were all iron ships propelled by steam. It was 1889, and Halifax harbour had changed sadly from the days when it was filled with Bluenose windjammers that were the slickest craft on the seas.

HALIFAX CARNIVAL

MID-SUMMER 1889.

ECHO

The 1889 midsummer carnival in Halifax was an extravaganza even fun-loving Montreal could never duplicate. It was the city's 140th birthday, and what a birthday party it was! Bands, floats, concerts, athletic competitions, contests, and the pièce de résistance – *a mock sea battle and storming of the famous Citadel.*

LANDSCAPE PAINTERS

The eighties were significant years in the development of Canadian artistic sensibilities. While young poets like Charles G.D. Roberts were beginning to celebrate the Canadian scene in an original style, the work of the young artists was expressing "a feeling its creator had of having roots in his native land and being a product of its soil," in the words of Homer Watson. For him and his fellow-Ontarians Horatio Walker and Lucius R. O'Brien, success in terms of recognition at home and internationally came in this period. The older O'Brien, primarily a water-colourist, was the force behind the establishment of the Royal Canadian Academy of Arts in 1880. Walker and Watson, who had worked in the '70s at Notman's photographic studio in Toronto run by John Fraser and Henry Sandham, would spend their long lives and artistic talents portraying the pastoral life of Quebec and Ontario.

Horatio Walker, born in Listowel, Ont., in 1858, spent his adult life on the Ile d'Orléans near Quebec. His water colours and oil paintings like Ave Maria *(right) idealized the traditional way of life of rural Québecois.*

The Laurentides *(1882) by Homer Watson of Doon, Ont. The farmland of southern Ontario and the Laurentian area were the primary subjects of Watson's paintbrush, and he won an international reputation for his sensitive depiction of the sombre Canadian landscape and pioneer life.*

Sunrise on the Saguenay *(1880) by Lucius R. O'Brien – his diploma-painting for the RCA's first exhibition in the new National Gallery at Ottawa. An enthusiastic patron of Canadian artists, Lord Lorne purchased three of O'Brien's paintings, which still hang today in Windsor Castle.*

CHAPTER EIGHT

"O CANADA"

Awake, my country, the hour of dreams is done!
Doubt not, nor dread the greatness of thy fate.

Charles G.D. Roberts, "An Ode for the Canadian Confederacy"

Two events serve to demonstrate the tenuous, earnest, promising, occasionally comic state of art and culture in Canada as the country moved into the 1880s. One took place in Toronto; its scene was spare and lonely and filled with yearning – a poetic occasion. The other, set in Quebec City, was noisy and public, with thousands on hand to celebrate it.

The first event occurred in 1880 at Trinity College. Archibald Lampman, a nineteen-year-old boy with a mop of dark brown hair flowing over his collar, sat through a night reading over and over again by candlelight a book of poetry, *Orion and Other Poems,* written by another young Canadian, Charles G. D. Roberts of Fredericton, New Brunswick. It was a night of enchantment and revelation for Lampman, and he expressed its magic a few years later.

Like most of the young fellows about me, I had been under the depressing conviction that we were situated hopelessly on the outskirts of civilization, where no art and no literature could be, and that it was useless to expect that anything great could be done by any of our companions, still more useless to expect that we could do it ourselves. I sat up most of the night reading and re-reading Orion *in a state of the wildest excitement and when I went to bed I could not sleep. It seemed to me a wonderful thing that such work could be done by a Canadian, by a young man, one of ourselves. It was like a voice from some new paradise of art, calling us to be up and doing.*

In the second tableau, set a few months earlier, Quebec City had gathered to greet the touring governor general and his wife, the Marquis of Lorne and Princess Louise. Calixa Lavallée, composer, conductor, musician *extraordinaire*, had organized for the occasion an assembly of three thousand vocalists and musicians from the choirs and orchestras of Quebec and other Canadian and American cities. He conducted them through a flawless programme of appropriately stirring musical works, leading to a mighty climax in his own cantata of welcome, a virtuoso feat of contrapuntal orchestration – nothing less than a simultaneous rendition of "God Save The Queen," "Vive La Canadienne" and "Comin' Through The Rye." The effect was stunning. The crowd hailed Lavallée's triumph, the musicians and singers were exalted, the Princess was overwhelmed and the Marquis appeared appreciatively stupefied – though not nearly as stupefied as Lavallée was a few days later. The civic committee that had retained him declined, with hand-wringing regret and pleading lack of funds, to pay him and his musicians. Lavallée's day of triumph left him several hundred dollars out of pocket.

Artistic societies began to flourish in the young nation in the eighties. This charming design announced an ambitious musical programme ending with a rousing "Vive La Canadienne."

Opposite page: *The autobiography of Egerton Ryerson, the man who started the* Methodist Book and Publishing House *in 1829, lies open in front of some of the firm's publications of the eighties under the imprint of William Briggs, Book Steward, 1879 to 1919. Titles reflect a growing emphasis on Canadian travel, history and fiction.*

Archibald Lampman
Classicist, Poet and Postal Clerk

The roots of poetry as an expression of the Canadian country and people saw their first growth in the eighties and took shape in the forms borrowed from the British and American traditions. For Archibald Lampman the sonnet was the form of expression for many of his finest lyrics. He was Ontario-born in 1861, and graduated from Toronto's Trinity College in Classics in 1882. His contemporaries, Roberts, Carman and Crawford, attempted to live by their writing, but he took a clerk's job with the Post Office Department and wrote poetry in his spare time, frequently escaping the stifling atmosphere of the office by walks and canoe trips in the surrounding countryside. His first book *Among the Millet* (1888), containing many poems descriptive of the Ottawa Valley, was well received as were his next two volumes published in the '90s. The last, *Alcyone*, was published posthumously; the rheumatic fever he'd suffered in his childhood brought untimely death in 1899.

Young men with artistic sensibilities as diverse as Lavallée's and Lampman's seemed to spring up everywhere in Canada in the 1880s. It was this decade that saw a determined beginning of a consistent native culture in the Dominion. It hardly matters now that much of the work produced by the new poets, painters and composers swung wildly between the precious stuff of lonely garrets and something that came closer to outrageous bombast, or even that the Canadian public didn't always rally in appreciation with its attention and its pocketbook. What is important now is the beginning – the birth of a creative culture.

Charles G. D. Roberts along with his cousin, Bliss Carman, and the young Archibald Lampman emerged as the first internationally admired Canadian poets. Lavallée, despite his instinct for the pompous, appeared as Canada's first all-round man of music, "a musician of original thought and progressive methods," according to the New York *Times*. And Madame Emma Albani of Chambly, Quebec, consolidated her career in the eighties as perhaps the greatest *diva* of the day. The Royal Canadian Academy of Arts was formed in 1880 and held its first show that year in Ottawa at the new National Gallery of Canada. Throughout the decade, painters like Horatio Walker, Lucius O'Brien and Homer Watson (the "Constable of Canada," in Oscar Wilde's judgement) exhibited works that were loosely grouped in a first Canadian school. The Royal Society, an organization promoting science and literature, got going in 1882. A year later Goldwin Smith founded the *Week*, a brilliant and outspoken journal ($3.00 a year, single copy 7¢) that quickly became the focus of literary and cultural life in Canada.

To many Canadians, this fresh burst of artistic activity was a matter for suspicion. Their image of Canadian society as earthy and egalitarian seemed somehow threatened, and they reacted with a certain amount of philistine carping. The Marquis of Lorne, who was a supremely cultivated gentleman and a driving force behind both the Royal Society and the Royal Academy, delivered a gently rebuking speech at the opening of the National Gallery's first show. "I believe," he said, "some gentlemen have been good enough to propose we should postpone the initiation of this institution for the present, and should wait for the short and moderate space of exactly one hundred years, and look forward to its incorporation in the year of grace 1980."

a man of letters

The detractors had their natural effect on the young artists' income – or lack of income. After his financial *débâcle* in Quebec City, Lavallée moved to Boston where he found steady work and plenty of money. Bliss Carman was another who eventually discovered recognition for his work, in monetary terms, in the United States. And Madame Albani had earned her reputation in Europe, complete with command performances at Windsor and Balmoral for Queen Victoria, before Canadian audiences were prepared to accept her. Painters like Watson and Walker made far more money in the early eighties retouching photographs in the studios of Messrs. Notman and Fraser of Montreal than they did from their paintings. (The Fraser of the partnership, John Fraser, was himself an important pioneer in landscape painting.) Canadian publishers, most of all, were notoriously stingy; they usually demanded that authors provide, before publication, subscription lists that would guarantee profitable sales of their work.

The publishers' reluctance made it all the more remarkable that Charles G. D. Roberts was able to carve out a career for himself as the first full-time all-round man of letters in Canadian literary history. Almost from his graduation *cum laude* from the University of New Brunswick in 1879,

94

Roberts – known to friends as Charles "God Damned" Roberts – made his living by writing poetry, short stories and criticism, and by editing, lecturing, teaching and staging dramatic recitations of his own poetry.

The life style that Roberts adopted introduced a new, livelier, mildly bohemian dimension to Canadian life. Like a transplanted Swinburne, he strode about Fredericton, and later Toronto, in homespun Norfolk knickers and a velvet coat. His appearance was so distinctive that a letter once reached him addressed only to "The man in the belted coat with the dog and the knotted stick who lives in Nova Scotia." When Oscar Wilde visited Fredericton in 1882, Roberts dutifully called on him at the Queens Hotel, and Wilde instantly recognized a kindred spirit. The two sat long into the night drinking gin and ginger beer, toasting the gods of Athens and Rome, and taking turns reading each other's poetry. When Wilde left, he told Roberts there was "no height in song beyond your reach." Matthew Arnold was an encouraging influence too; when Roberts was editing the *Week* in Toronto in 1883, Arnold encountered him at a party given by Goldwin Smith, threw his arms around him and announced, "This is the boy I wanted to meet."

convinced nationalists

But, for all his posturing, Roberts found his greatest poetic inspiration in his own country's landscape and in the Canadians who lived and worked in it. So did the generation of writers he influenced. In their best moments, when they put aside their romanticized notions about sylvan fields and damsels and heroic Greeks, Bliss Carman, Archibald Lampman, Isabella Valancy Crawford, Duncan Campbell Scott and a handful of others revealed themselves as the most convinced nationalists of the day.

THE MELANCHOLY MUSE

Isabella Valancy Crawford

"One of the first to translate our still mysterious melancholy dominion" into poetry was Valancy Crawford, who published a first verse collection at her own expense in 1884, just three years before her sudden death. Born in Dublin in 1850, she was eight when her family emigrated to Ontario. Her father practised medicine in the villages of Paisley, Lakefield and Peterborough, where she absorbed the experiences of pioneer life in the backwoods along with a thorough home education in classical and modern literature. The two long narrative poems in her book *Old Spookses' Pass, Malcolm's Katie and Other Poems* show a style unequalled in its colour and originality, capturing the effects of the brooding monster of Nature on an emerging civilization and mythologizing the Canadian environment.

from **Malcolm's Katie**

The mighty morn strode laughing up the land,
And Max, the laborer and the lover, stood
Within the forest's edge, beside a tree,
The mossy king of all the woody tribes,
Whose clatt'ring branches rattl'd, shuddering,
As the bright axe cleav'd moon-like thro' the air,
Waking strange thunders, rousing echoes link'd
From the full, lion-throated roar, to sighs
Stealing on dove-wings thro' the distant aisles.
Swift fell the axe, swift follow'd roar on roar,
Till the bare woodland bellow'd in its rage,
As the first-slain slow toppl'd to his fall.

* * * * *

It was not all his own, the axe-stirr'd waste.
In these new days men spread about the earth
With wings at heel–and now the settler hears,
While yet his axe rings on the primal woods,
The shrieks of engines rushing o'er the wastes;
Nor parts his kind to hew his fortunes out.
And as one drop glides down the unknown rock
And the bright-threaded stream leaps after it
With welded billions, so the settler finds
His solitary footsteps beaten out
With the quick rush of panting, human waves
Upheav'd by throbs of angry poverty,
And driven by keen blasts of hunger, from
Their native strands – so stern, so dark, so dear!

* * * * *

Then came smooth-coated men, with eager eyes,
And talk'd of steamers on the cliff-bound lakes;
And iron tracks across the prairie lands;
And mills to crush the quartz of wealthy hills;
And mills to saw the great, wide-arm'd trees;
And mills to grind the singing stream of grain;
And with such busy clamor mingled still
The throbbing music of the bold, bright Axe –
The steel tongue of the Present, and the wail
Of falling forests – voices of the Past.

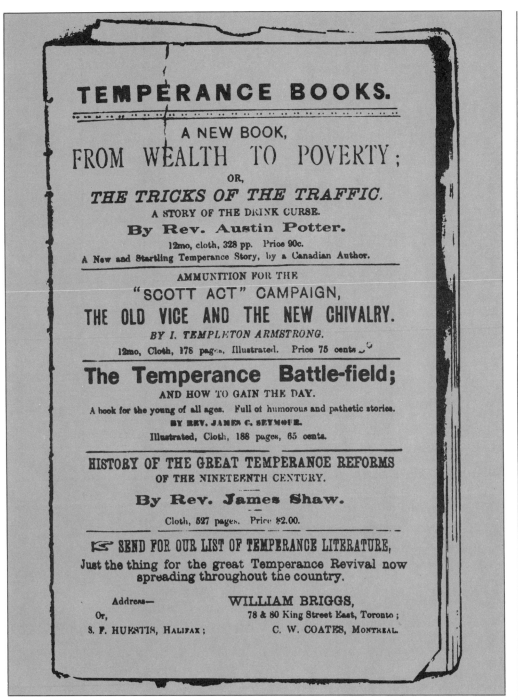

William Briggs kept the Methodist Book and Publishing House firmly behind the forces of temperance.

Roberts rhapsodized about the primitive, difficult life of New Brunswick farmers, but also wrote other poems with patriotic titles – "An Ode for the Canadian Confederacy," "Canada," and "Collect for Dominion Day." Bliss Carman likewise drew inspiration for his finest work from New Brunswick's land and people. Archibald Lampman, whose daytime hours were spent at a dull grey job in the Post Office Department in Ottawa would spend the evenings with a group of friends discussing, in the Fabian style, worldly topics like women's rights, the conflict between science and religion, the distastefulness of party politics and routine church-going. They formed the core of the first literary intelligentsia in the capital. Still Lampman found his happiest and most powerful poetic subjects in the nature and beauty of the Ottawa Valley.

a sense of pride

Sometimes the nationalist sentiment got out of hand. William Douw Lighthall, Montreal lawyer and writer, edited *Songs of the Great Dominion* in 1889. In the introduction to the collection of breathtakingly optimistic poems about Canada's history and future, Lighthall exulted that Canada was shaped by "the noblest epic migration the world has ever seen," that in the future she was "to clarify for the whole British Empire its task of leading the advance towards a Federation of Mankind." Still, even in an exaggerated idealization of what the country should be, the new poets were offering Canadians some sense of pride and awe in the vast and overpowering country they inhabited, and some awareness of themselves as Canadians.

No one could make the same claim about the fiction of the decade – it was anything but Canadian. And yet Canadians read an astonishing number of novels. "Book consumption," publisher

George Doran wrote of the 1880s, "is higher per capita than in any other country of the world with the possible exception of Australia. Good bookshops are to be found in every town of more than one thousand inhabitants. Toronto . . . has at least a score of real book stores owned and operated by highly intelligent booksellers." Magazines like the *Week* and *Toronto Saturday Night* (which began publication in 1887) regularly carried serialized novels; most newspapers printed short stories in daily editions; and store racks and news-stands were lined with mass-produced fiction papers designed after the English penny-weeklies, that sold for six cents apiece.

This bonanza of stories and novels, at least at the beginning of the decade, reflected little that was Canadian. Home-grown fiction writers were few in number. And they received minimal encouragement from Canadian publishers; William Briggs, whose Methodist Book and Publishing House was generally considered most partial to Canadian poets and writers, produced one original novel per year.

Most fiction was imported in American magazines like *Harper's, Atlantic,* and *Scribner's Monthly,* and in British journals like *Blackwood's, Illustrated London News, Macmillan's Monthly,* and *Temple Bar.* "British magazines," said the *Week,* which, in the custom of the period, reviewed magazines as thoroughly as it reviewed books, "cannot compete in numbers, liveliness, variety and price with the American. . . . The Americans sell 100 to 1 against the British." And, among the foreign novels that flooded Canada, the Americans outsold the British, primarily by underselling them.

In the late 1870s, a few unorthodox publishers in the cities of the eastern United States effected a publishing revolution when they began to mass-produce novels in paper-covered editions that sold at five, ten or twenty cents. A group of Canadians,

as it happened, had a hand in this paperback revolution. The Belford brothers and James Clarke from Toronto, John Lovell from Montreal and Norman Munro from Halifax, all of them businessmen with a sharp eye for a dollar, moved to the United States and sliced off profitable pieces of the cut-rate book industry. They printed in runs of thousands and shipped back home libraries of ten-cent paperback books, thus fashioning careers for themselves as the first successful Canadian print entrepreneurs.

These paperbacks were pot-boilers of no special literary merit, but the books did have the distinction of dealing with the North American scene. They were rich in the local colour of New England, the American South and especially the Far West of cowboy adventurers.

an important influence

The first Canadians to turn out similar popular fiction were obscure novelists like Roger Pocock and Clive Phillips-Wolley. They adapted the Canadian milieu to the popular-novel formula and had the satisfaction of seeing Canadian publishers eventually place their novels in print. Toronto publishers, acting as agents for New York firms, often issued their own editions of successful American novels that happened to have been written by Canadians. Thus, as early as the eighties, Canadians were recognizing their own talent, slender though the talent may have been, only after it had been recognized elsewhere.

But the most important influence of the popular North American-oriented novels was on young readers. Twenty years later the first generation of writers to manifest a decisively Canadian point of view in their own work – Ralph Connor, Nellie McClung, Lucy Maud Montgomery – drew their themes to an important degree from the six-cent weeklies and paperback thrillers they read growing

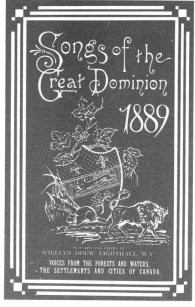

"The poets whose songs fill this book are voices cheerful with the consciousness of young might, public wealth, and heroism" – the opening sentence of William Douw Lighthall's collection of Canadian poetry published in 1889. Lighthall too turned his hand to verse, although a lawyer by profession. Born in 1857, he lived almost a century in the "Great Dominion" he lauded.

Calixa Lavallée
Nationaliste Manqué

The man who composed the stirring music for the country's national anthem rejected his home and native land shortly after the first performance of "O Canada" in 1880. It wasn't the first time Calixa Lavallée had gone to the U.S. In his late teens, he had served in the Northern armies during the Civil War–as a bandsman, following a brief stint with a touring theatrical troupe from New Orleans. Son of a Verchères, Que., blacksmith-turned-organ-builder, Lavallée had been a child prodigy–organist at the St. Hyacinthe Cathedral in 1852 at the age of eleven. After his youthful rebellion he made Canada home base in the '60s and '70s but also conducted opera in New York and studied in Paris. In 1880 "O Canada" received enthusiastic response but not his plan to establish a music conservatory. Thereupon he moved to Boston, but he continued to compose operatic works until his death in '91.

up in the eighties. Fortunately also, their books shared one other property with the early novels– they were all, in their different days, best-sellers.

The tug and haul between Victorian high-mindedness and the natural North American vulgarity that Canadians endured in their literature caused just as much friction and variation in their approach to music in the 1880s. The contrasts were strong and frequently comic as Canadians lurched from awkward musical amateurism to stern, European-style professionalism.

opera and band music

Opera enjoyed huge popularity in eastern Canada, especially when foreign troupes performed. Anything European, Canadians decided, had to be uplifting. In the winter of 1889-90, Torontonians patronized fifty-six performances of twenty-six touring operas, ten of them grand operas, a season that far surpassed opera activity in the city half a century later. The audiences treated the touring companies with appropriate reverence, but the companies didn't always return the compliment. For them, Canada remained the sticks and it was a common occurrence for the advertised stars not to bother showing up on stage, or even in the city. In April 1880, *Rose Belford's Canadian Monthly* pronounced the Strakosch Italian Opera Company a "fraud" for just that reason, and the following month the French Opera Bouffe Company failed to produce, as advertised, its three leading singers. That time, Toronto's audience did react in a less than reverent manner. "The curtain," reported the *Monthly*, "fell amid some very earnest hissing, an incident almost unprecedented, we believe, in the performance of Italian Opera in this city."

On their own, Canadians were a remarkably musical people in the last years of the century; it was in all ways an era of ambitious do-it-yourself musical activity. Edgar Dewdney's first request to

Sir John A. Macdonald, after he was appointed lieutenant-governor of the North-West Territories, was to have a grand piano shipped to Government House. "There are," Dewdney wrote the prime minister, "over the average of musical people in Regina." Regina formed a Musical Club in 1882, a Musical and Literary Society by 1886, a fourteen-piece brass band the same year, a Glee Club and a second Musical Society in 1888 and a Choral Society in 1889. In Vancouver, the Coal Harbour Bachelor's Quadrille Club, established in 1886, provided serious musical entertainment. In Toronto the Quartette Club, all local talent, presented twelve fortnightly Monday Popular Concerts in the 1885-6 season.

Quebec boasted most of all of its band music. It was the talents of three men – Calixa Lavallée, Arthur Lavigne, a music-store owner and song publisher from Quebec City, and the famous band master, Joseph Vezina – that raised band music to a distinct and highly popular music form. Concerts of several bands massed into one huge orchestra became ritual events throughout Quebec, usually with Lavallée or Vezina conducting. The most historic concert took place in Quebec City on St. Jean-Baptiste Day in 1880 when a massed band under Vezina's baton presented a song dashed off by Lavallée a few days earlier in an hour of inspiration, and published a few weeks later, an instant hit – "O Canada."

amateurs and professionals

But it was oratorio – choral performances of sacred music by giant choirs ranged row on row with "*alti, soprani, bassi* and *tenori*," – that was most typical of Canadian music of the decade. And, indeed, oratorio best reflected the emotions and attitudes that Canadians brought to all of their culture in those years. Oratorio, like Canada's artistic yearnings, tended to be spectacular and grand and obviously high-minded. And it did not disturb Canadians that it was also often derivative and slightly comic.

There was, for instance, the Grand Festival of 1886, the brainchild of Toronto's determinedly ambitious Philharmonic Society. The Philharmonic had been presenting concerts since 1872, and by 1886, when its orchestra had collected sixty-nine players, it decided to launch its most daring presentation, the greatest musical event yet presented in Canada. For three evening performances and one matinee, it offered, in one magnificent gathering, a festival of a thousand choristers, twelve hundred children's voices and an augmented orchestra of one hundred instruments. All these performers were Canadian but, as a crowning touch, the Philharmonic brought in two foreign stars, the famous European singers, Max Heinrich and Lilli Lehmann.

a tentative beginning

Alas, despite the stars and the masses of talent, the overflow audiences and the ambition of the occasion, it failed. There wasn't enough symphonic music on the programme, there was insufficient orchestra rehearsal and too much emphasis on the spectacular. In Lilli Lehmann's words, "It was extremely ludicrous. . . . An elderly conductor knew so little about the Mozart score that I called him, in English, in the presence of the committee, a veritable ass, after my aria from the *Entführung*, and he did not take umbrage but tried to excuse himself."

And that incident, in a microcosm, described the state of Canadian art in the 1880s. It was ardent, but frequently inept; elaborate, but not always adventurous; vaguely aware of its native power, but too anxious to measure itself by foreign standards. It was at an early, tentative, promising beginning.

The St. Jean-Baptiste Day parade on June 24 in Quebec always drew crowds to cheer the bands.

Working under the statutory labour laws of the late 19th century, these men are hauling crushed stone to build roads by their farms in the Peterborough area.

CHAPTER NINE

THE SONS OF TOIL

True men all must toil and drudge.

Alexander McLachlan, "Acres of your Own"

There is nothing, no memoir, no membership record, no footnote, to suggest that William Collins ever joined the Holy and Noble Order of the Knights Of Labor. But Collins, a machinist from Hamilton, Ontario, and something of an amateur philosopher, was just the sort of workingman the Knights had in mind when they launched their gallant and sensible crusade on behalf of Canadian labour through the 1880s.

Collins was, so he said himself, "a diligent reader of Henry George," the contemporary American political scientist who preached that all men had equal rights to the fruits of the earth, and he was a canny organizer of his own resources. Even though, as he said, "to a fairly cultivated taste, a man who has to live on the earnings of a mere machinist has to practice denial," he was able to put aside enough savings to retire at the age of fifty. It helped that he had no children and that "I was exceedingly fortunate in my matrimonial adventure." So he passed the days in retirement reading his Henry George and pondering the awful realization that workingmen like himself were not taking in a fair share of the benefits that the growing industrialization of Canada was undoubtedly offering.

When the Royal Commission on the Relations of Labor and Capital, appointed by Sir John A. Macdonald, came to Hamilton in 1887, William Collins was waiting and ready to express his puzzlement.

There is some hocus-pocus about this that I cannot exactly get at the bottom of myself. I feel somehow or other that the employee is run out of this question – he is not considered. He is just a pawn in the game, and there is where the trouble lies, and until the employee awakens, it will always lie there.

Exactly right, the Knights of Labor echoed. Bravo William Collins! The workingman *was* cheated and downtrodden.

Thanks in large part to Macdonald's National Policy, offering tariff protection to Canadian manufacturing, central Canada had begun to boom with industrialization. The fresh prosperity created a new white-collar and managerial class but confined workingmen to an existence that was short on money, culture, fun and future. From 1881 to 1891, Canada's industrial labour force increased by 41 percent; in the same period, the worker's average wage in most industries rose by amounts measured in cents, hovering around a figure of less than ten dollars per week. The workingman was victimized, and it was the Knights of Labor, above all organizations, who first moved to his aid.

This prize list cover romanticizes the site of the Toronto Industrial Exhibition, the eighth annual extravaganza since the municipal politicians expanded the idea of an agricultural fair to include industrial, trade and even artisitc organizations. The Knights of Labor took part in the procession.

FIRE!

In cities toward the end of the century, fire-fighting organizations evolved from voluntary community associations–everyone was expected to help man the bucket-brigade. (Top) Fire department members pulling a fire reel through Victoria's streets c. 1887; (bottom) horse-drawn fire engines and uniformed fire fighters in front of Winnipeg's #2 Station in 1884.

The Knights convened an inaugural Canadian meeting on an autumn evening in 1881 in the unfinished Canada Life Assurance Building of Hamilton (a city, at the time, of 35,961 citizens and 52 factories). The Knights, who resembled the Masons in their devotion to elaborate ritual, secret handshakes and high-falutin' titles (Venerable Sage, Master Workman), were already twelve years old in the United States. The Canadian off-spring quickly spread across central Canada and into Manitoba and the Maritimes, boasting at least 12,253 members in 168 Local Assemblies at its peak in 1887. Its membership was drawn from all occupations, taking in every anxious, underpaid labouring man, whether skilled or unskilled (excluding only bankers, lawyers, gamblers and those who turned a dollar at trade in alcoholic beverages). It proclaimed its intention "to secure for all workers the full enjoyment of the wealth they create and sufficient leisure in which to develop their intellectual, moral and social faculties." Through the eighties, the Knights rose to prominence by preaching all kinds of heresies – the end of child labour, the use of arbitration between employer and employee, the practice of abstinence from liquor, and the prompt improvement of the conditions of industrial labour.

the typical workingman

Working conditions were cruel, enough to kill a man's body and soul. Few factory employees were as lucky – or as resourceful – as William Collins, that sturdy survivor. If we looked for the typical workingman of the 1880s, we'd probably settle for the employee of a Toronto tannery who laboured sixty hours a week. Late on Saturday afternoons he took home eight dollars to the narrow, one-storey frame cottage he rented in the St. Andrews Ward of the city's downtown. Eight dollars? It didn't go far in a week. Five dollars for food, two dollars and a quarter on rent, a quarter's worth of fuel, thirty cents for carfare, postage, newspapers and other odds and ends, another dime for tobacco, and that left ten cents between the family and hard times. "When health gives way," Eli Massey, a Montreal cigar-maker, told the Royal Commission, "we must necessarily contract debts."

modest comforts

Our tannery worker's rented home, where he lived with his wife and two children, offered modest comforts. The privy was out back, and the well gave murky drinking water. No wonder – in one year, 1887, the city hauled seventeen tons of human excrement out of St. Andrews. Inside, the cottage was divided into three rooms – a kitchen for cooking, eating and socializing and two other chambers for sleeping and seeking a private corner. The furniture was rudimentary and so was the menu. Bread, tea, potatoes, molasses, porridge, milk, butter and a bit of beef or mutton. The shelves held one book, a Bible, and a stack of back copies of the *Toronto News*, a four-page evening daily that cheered workingmen by its advocacy of "simple democracy and good sense."

For all the plainness of his hearth, the tannery worker found pleasure in his family. Work in the factories had replaced the craftsman's traditional custom of working at home. Thus a man's house, however humble, became a refuge, and the family, however hard-pressed, grew into a social and leisure unit. Picnics, circuses, swimming in Toronto Bay, excursions to Toronto Island – whatever the family embarked on together had to be inexpensive or free, but at least a man had familial companionship to lean on.

Neither family nor the workingman's other companion, booze, could entirely distract our tannery man from the burden of his job. The hours weighed heaviest, 60 of them per week in the

By 1880 when the Bell Telephone Company of Canada was incorporated, telephone lines were connecting major towns and cities in Eastern Canada, and the job of telephone-line repairman had come into existence.

**Sandford Fleming
Midwife to Standard Time**

When Sandford Fleming stepped off his immigrant ship in 1845, at 18, a Toronto cleric advised him to return to Scotland, as there were no "great works" left undone in the colony. But in the next 70 years Fleming, as railway builder, scientist, diplomat, author and university chancellor, found and succeeded brilliantly at a tremendous variety of great works. He surveyed Canada coast to coast for four railways, including the CPR. Midwife to world standard time and the Pacific telegraph cable, he produced Canada's first large-scale surveyor's maps and designed our first postage stamp. Although he never attended university, he revered higher learning to the extent that he was more honoured to be chosen chancellor of Queen's than to be knighted by Queen Victoria in 1897.

tannery, but it could have been worse. The men who unloaded ships in Halifax sometimes worked 35 hours at a stretch, and policemen in Montreal pounded their beats 98 hours a week for 92 cents per day. Whatever the length, a working day frequently drained its servants. "It is the long hours," a Carling brewery employee of London, Ontario, complained in 1887, "that take away my time, air, sun, light and probably my promise."

child labour

And with all his other worries, the tannery worker fretted most deeply over his twelve-year-old son who had just begun employment in a nearby box factory. Children seemed special victims of industrialization. A shoe factory in London, Ontario, paid thirteen-year-old girls one cent for every sole they made – and fined them four cents for each defective sole. Fortier's cigar factory in Montreal maintained a "black hole" in its cellar where the foreman locked disobedient ten-year-old cigar-rollers as punishment. Twelve-year-old Joseph Lefebre, at work beside his machine in an Ottawa mill, slipped and, before he could stand up, the axle of a wheel crushed his right arm and leg. The boss gave him ten dollars, and Joseph was officially listed as an "Invalid" and therefore unemployable. Then there was the government inspector who returned from a trip to a factory in Merritton, Ontario, and reported on the state of the town's adolescents. "Children go to work so young, have so little outdoors exercise and inhale so much dust that it weakens them and you find more old men and women here at thirty than in most places at fifty."

The governments of Canada and the provinces took steps to help working children, as well as their mothers and fathers, but they moved on tip-toe. In 1886 Ontario's premier, Sir Oliver Mowat, proclaimed the country's first Factory Act, setting standards for industrial safety and establishing minimum age limits for factory employment– twelve for boys and fourteen for girls. Employers and parents had little trouble evading the Act's strictures. Also in 1886, on the eve of a federal election and with a slight tip of the hat to the labour vote, Sir John A. appointed the Royal Commission "for the purpose of enquiring into and reporting on all questions arising out of the conflicts of labor and capital." The Commission, with a couple of labour representatives, held sessions from Windsor, Ontario, to Cape Breton, Nova Scotia, generating the odd spark of publicity (newspapers turned the "black hole" of Fortier's cigar factory into a juicy item), but it effected no substantial reforms. If change were to occur in Canada's industrial life, it wouldn't come from the politicians nor from the manufacturers, those champions of rugged individualism. Labour, it remained clear, must initiate its own crusade.

fuelling the labour cause

At which point, the Knights of Labor entered the picture. Individual trades – printers and plasterers, stonecutters and bakers – formed themselves into units for discussion and bargaining, and so did larger union groups. The first meeting of the Canadian Trades And Labor Congress took place in December 1883 at the Dufferin Hall in Toronto. But it was the Knights, idealistic and even quixotic though they were, who dominated the labour scene. The Knights' strength did not last past the end of the decade; one principle that doomed the organization eventually was their reluctance to strike. Still, along the way, they circulated ideas, standards and moral precepts that fuelled the labour cause for years to come.

In their grandest dreams, the Knights wanted to convert workmen into replicas of William Collins – thoughtful men who eschewed the relief

A hearty crew of lumberjacks in an Ottawa Valley camp show off the tools of their trade–and the camp mascot's litter of pups (note the one in the cook's arms at left).

SEASONAL EMPLOYMENT

One of the first jobs lumberjacks had to undertake was the building of the road through the forests into the camp, usually begun in early winter.

Agricultural machinery and methods had become more sophisticated by the '80s but "stumping"–the final stage of clearing land–required lots of manual labour.

The apparatus manned by dock workers on Halifax's waterfront below Citadel Hill was for weighing hogsheads (large casks containing from 50 to 120 gallons) of fish.

Refrigeration, just developing in the '80s, hadn't yet replaced the ice-cutters. Here, men hoist onto a sleigh huge blocks of ice sawn from the frozen river.

of liquor and turned instead to culture and the printed word. Thus, the Knights founded newspapers and organized libraries, inspired co-op enterprises (a knitting factory in Norwich, Ontario, grocery stores in Montreal) and launched lecture tours by righteous and dull men who proclaimed the virtues of the well-examined life. Alas, working people weren't ready for the Knights' best intentions. "Wage earners," declared the *Labor Advocate,* a newspaper voice of the Knights, in one of its last cranky editorials, "are so stupidly blind to their own interests that they can't see the advantages of having a lively, outspoken journal to plead their cause."

strikes and lock-outs

The workers weren't so much "stupidly blind" as they were dead tired. It was enervating for our typical Toronto tannery hand to drag himself out of the factory, full of grey air, to the Mechanics' Institute reading room on Adelaide Street where the atmosphere was equally forbidding. It took a ferociously determined man, someone like William Collins, to resist the easier appeal of home or tavern. And the Knights' vision of enlightened workers began to be shaken by the harsh everyday realities.

The Toronto Street Railway strike of 1886 represented another blow to the Knights' dreams. The TSR was a private outfit, licensed to maintain the city's transportation services. A self-made Irish-Canadian millionaire, Senator Frank Smith, made it show a profit, partly by taking a stingy line with his employees. Drivers and conductors earned a mere nine dollars for a six-day week of fourteen-hour days on the cars. In exasperation, three employees joined the Knights of Labor. Smith promptly fired the three. Just as promptly, on Wednesday, March 9, 1886, one hundred and thirty-three workers marched smartly up Yonge Street to the Knights' headquarters in the Arcade Building and took out memberships. They were, they announced, on strike.

Smith recruited new employees and attempted to carry on. Amazingly, most ordinary citizens– and at least one extraordinary citizen – took the workers' side. "You have by your own act produced this trouble," Smith read in a letter fired off to him by Mayor William Howland, the first authentic reformer elected to that lofty office in Toronto, "having in the face of the knowledge of the results locked out a large body of your men, not on account of any claim for higher wages, but simply for exercising a legal liberty in joining a lawful body or society." Many Torontonians took more direct action, gathering in solid masses to prevent Smith's cars from leaving their King Street barns. On Friday, March 10, the anti-TSR demonstrators threatened to riot; nervous police prepared to charge the mob when suddenly a company of militiamen in scarlet swung on the scene. Both police and civilians fell back. Who had summoned the soldiers? As it turned out, no one. The militiamen were returning, via King Street, from a dead comrade's funeral. The threat of riot passed.

a daring enterprise

Senator Smith capitulated and hired back the striking employees, but at the same old threadbare wages, with the Knights raising no fuss. Two months later, the employees began lobbying for a shorter work day. Smith responded in familiar style by firing men for minor infractions. This time, the workers attempted to set up their own city transportation system in competition with the TSR. The Knights rallied to the daring enterprise, helping to collect 200 horses from its own Teamsters & Carters Assembly, a dozen omnibuses from workers in nearby Oshawa, money donations

John J. McLaughlin
The Teetotaler's Brewer

After Jack McLaughlin took the gold medal at the College of Pharmacy in Toronto in 1886, he went off to New York to work as a chemist's assistant. That very year, the Esteemed Brain Tonic and Intellectual Beverage, later known as Coca Cola, was launched and McLaughlin became interested in the new business of soft drinks (soda water had been around for a century). The eldest son of Robert McLaughlin, the Oshawa carriage-maker whose firm expanded rapidly in the '80s, Jack inherited some of his father's business acumen. Back in Toronto in 1888, he set up a small establishment for the bottling of mineral waters, moved in 1890 to a new plant on Sherbourne St. (where the firm remained until 1965). In 1904 McLaughlin's Pale Dry Ginger Ale adopted the trade name Canada Dry and, in the twenties, the slogan The Champagne of Ginger Ales.

"NEVER BEFORE WAS CANADA SO PROSPEROUS AS IT IS TO-DAY."

A recurring figure in J.W. Bengough's cartoons in Grip *was the "hard times" tramp. Here in an 1886 cartoon he uses a Gilbert and Sullivan "What! Never?" to point up the cruel difference between real conditions for the working man and the politicians' claims of prosperity.*

from other labour groups (Plasterers' Union: $200).

But events ran against the renegade transportation system. On June 20, an engulfing fire broke out at the old Dominion Bolt Company factory where the workers had set up their stables. Many horses perished. Perhaps most crippling of all, the public failed to back the striking workers this time; citizens were reacting at least partly to the Haymarket Riot in Chicago on May 4 when someone had set off a bomb, killing seven policemen. "The man who organizes a strike should be sent to penitentiary," preached a prominent Toronto evangelist, the Reverend Sam Small, echoing much of the city's middle-class sentiment, "and as for the man who leads a boycott, the only fit jewellery is a ball and chain." The workers' transportation system collapsed. With the Knights looking on helplessly from the sidelines, Senator Smith carried on business at the old stand, paying his usual rates for the usual long, cruel day of work.

The Knights held on as a voice in the labour movement for a few more years. They had a majority of delegates in the Trades And Labor Congress of Canada as late as 1894, but clearly the eighties had been their period of strength. The

unions that began to take up the cause differed from the Knights in two fundamental ways: they were more militant and less devoted to moral uplift; and they organized themselves by crafts and trades, rather than as a broad, all-inclusive group, through which they could exert more concentrated pressure on the bosses.

The Knights had stood for humanitarianism and respectability, two useful and rare commodities, but as the decade ended, it remained questionable whether they had guided Canada's working people very far along the way to a finer, more generous material state. William Collins, the machinist and sage from Hamilton, was undoubtedly on the mark when he tried to sum up the workers' position for the members of the Royal Commission on the Relations of Labor and Capital:

"Now it would be all right if the whole community equally benefitted – I do not go in for the laboring classes enjoying all the benefits – but I wish the working people to enjoy their portion. I am prepared to assert here or anywhere that the working people as a class do not enjoy those rights."

And they would not for several decades to come.

Right: *Pedlars still travelled through city streets and from town to village selling their wares in the eighties.*

THE COUNTRY AS IT WAS AND IS

The publication venture of the decade, *Picturesque Canada*, an illustrated survey of "the country as it was and is" in 1882. Published as a serial with thirty-six issues and sold only by subscription, the work provides unparallelled glimpses of the daily life of our ancestors. George M. Grant was literary editor and author of many sections; Lucius O'Brien, art editor; the Marquis of Lorne, patron.

George Monro Grant was the logical choice to edit Picturesque Canada. *In 1873 he had published* Ocean to Ocean, *a classic travel narrative of his trip across Canada with Sandford Fleming. Born in Nova Scotia in 1835, Grant was a Presbyterian minister (moderator in 1899), principal of Queen's University from 1877 until his death in 1902, and a charter member of the Royal Society of Canada in 1882.*

PICTURESQUE CANADA

The illustrations for *Picturesque Canada* were all made from woodcut engravings, in turn made from the original oil or water colour paintings or pencil sketches of over fifty artists. Lucius O'Brien became the art editor in 1880, the year he was also elected president of the Royal Canadian Academy of Arts which he'd helped to organize. He painted many of the works reproduced, travelling through every province during the four-year publication period. Fred Schell, O'Brien's colleague at Belden Brothers of Toronto who published the series, was the other major contributor of paintings; in fact he went on to Australia to carry out a similar publishing venture. The artists viewed the country and the people with a gentle eye–none of the harsh realities of life are pictured in the two collected volumes. The text, prepared by George M. Grant and nineteen other writers, recounts in an affectionate way the history and the folktales of the regions of Canada.

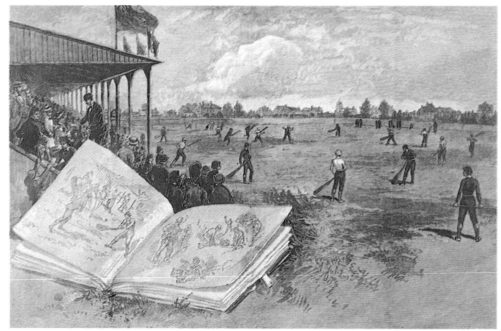

A grandstand crowd cheers on its favourite lacrosse team, and the artist records various action poses.

The Marquis of Lorne and Princess Louise became competent skaters while at Government House.

Overenthusiastic spectators risked a dunking in Toronto harbour as they hailed sculling competitors.

The idea of setting aside "a public park and a pleasure ground for the benefit, advantage and enjoyment of the people of Canada" was quite new in the '80's, but the government took tentative steps culminating in the Rocky Mountains Park Act of 1887. Active behind the scenes had been the CPR's Van Horne, envisioning trainloads of eager tourists. In the spring of the following year, the stately Banff Springs Hotel (right) was open for business. In the Illustrated London News, the curative powers of the springs were also featured (top).

CHAPTER TEN

THAT COLONY~A DANGEROUS NUISANCE

*I am having charming audiences . . . the
Canadians are very appreciative people . . .*

Oscar Wilde, from Halifax, 1882

The image that an English newspaper reader, frowning over the London *Times* in his favourite London club, entertained of Canada in 1880 hardly flattered Canadians. "That *colony*," according to John Walter, the brilliant and querulous editor of the *Times*, was "a dangerous nuisance," bound to involve Britain in unnecessary rows with the United States. Walter scorned Canada's "desperate loyalty" to Victoria and all things English, and his attitude dominated his paper. When the *Times* took notice of Canada at all, it displayed, in the words of Governor General Lorne, "sneering indifference and superciliousness."

And Canadians whose business brought them in contact with England often did little to counter their image as bumpkins. The major item of Canadian news among English gossips wasn't the CPR but the comic adventures of Sir Alexander Tilloch Galt. As for the railroad – "Jumbo, the big elephant recently bought by Barnum," George Stephen wrote back to Canada in disgust, "is a matter of ten times more interest to London than twenty colonies." But Alexander Galt, Canada's High Commissioner in London, was a different matter.

Galt had married his deceased wife's sister, a union that was, in the eyes of British law, technically illegal and, in the eyes of Queen Victoria, morally abhorrent. In Canada, only the Church of England opposed such marriages and the Canadian parliament was debating an act to legalize them (an act popularly known as "the Bill for the abolition of aunts") just at the time Galt was leaving for England. In Britain, the House of Lords defeated by a resounding majority a similar measure, introduced by the Prince of Wales in 1879, and as matters stood, Queen Victoria loudly and publicly refused to receive Lady Galt at court.

The Marquis of Lorne intervened on the poor lady's behalf. He himself didn't hold a particularly glowing opinion of Lady Galt's charms. "Mount-Edgecumbe (the Lord Chamberlain) cannot be supposed to know anything about a lady," he wrote to an English friend, referring to Lady Galt, "who had been very stay-at-home, low church and uninteresting." Still, Lorne finally arrived at a solution and persuaded the Prince of Wales to obtain a special dispensation from his mother on the tenuous ground that the marriage had taken place in the United States, where anything was thinkable.

A band of rivermen from Canada offered England a similarly unappealing picture of Canadians – rough-edged, mannerless, the sort who'd make dismal companions. They came forward,

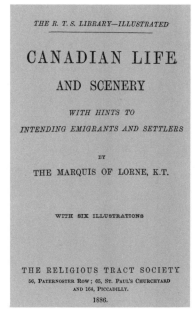

The Marquis of Lorne was a most energetic promoter even after his tour of duty in Rideau Hall. His travel guide with "hints to intending emigrants" was published in England in 1886.

FROM CANADA TO KHARTOUM

Dressed in their best and solemnly posed on the steps of Ottawa's Parliament Buildings, the Canadian contingent to the Sudan (below) resembles a convention of business men rather than an expeditionary force. But General Garnet Wolseley (right) needed the help of Canadian boatmen to navigate the Nile and relieve Khartoum in Aug. 1884, and the force carried out its service with distinction, if not sobriety.

gallantly enough, to assist Britain in rescuing the legendary General Charles Gordon and his garrison at Khartoum in the Sudan. The British War Office decided to send a force under General Sir Garnet Wolseley up the Nile to attack the fanatical Mahdi and his army of dervishes surrounding Khartoum. Wolseley, who had served in Canada, decided that the only men with enough strength and savvy to contend with the fierce rapids of the Nile were the latter-day voyageurs he had encountered on the rivers of the Canadian wilderness. Accordingly Wolseley recruited a troop of 373 Canadians, most of them loggers or shantymen—and almost all of them hard drinkers. "It was decidedly what they call a cheery crowd," the governor general's secretary concluded after he had spent the day of the troop's departure from Ottawa helping to round up recruits "who missed the train, owing to their having imbibed too freely."

the Nile contingent

The men lived up to this description at every port they hit on the way to Egypt. At Sydney, Nova Scotia, "one young man entered a school house," the Toronto *Globe* reported, "delivered a speech to the children and attempted to mash the teacher." At Gibraltar, two Indian brothers from Montreal "gave a lot of trouble being drunk and quarrelsome," recorded the troop's commanding officer, Lt.-Col. Frederick Denison of Toronto. "Six water-police assisted by four or five civilians tried to arrest them but failed." The story was the same at Alexandria and at Cairo, and it had been the same at sea, since the men had taken the precaution of smuggling aboard enough corn whisky to see them across the Atlantic.

Once the voyageurs reached the Nile, they served with distinction. They pulled through the rugged rapids, manipulated around the boulder-strewn shallows of the southern Nile – and it wasn't their fault that the rescue force arrived three days after the fall of Khartoum and the death of Gordon. But on the homeward journey, they resumed their old free-and-easy ways with the bottle. They livened up every city they passed through; and on the passenger ship that carried them the final leg of the trip from the port of Queenston in Ireland, the unhappy captain complained, "the men were drunk all the way from Queenston to Halifax." This display, many Englishmen grumbled, was just the sort of behaviour one would expect from Canadians.

favourable publicity, please

The Marquis of Lorne set out to change England's attitude to Canada and to Canadians. When Lorne first visited Canada on a private tour in 1866, he hadn't been especially fond of the place; "Toronto is too dull for words," he told his diary. But during his tour of duty as governor general, he developed a deep affection for Canada. He came to resent the virtual news blackout in England. "If we were rowdies and knocked the Constitution to pieces every five minutes like the Australians," he wrote to his father, "we should have dozens of specials." He wanted more publicity for Canada in Britain, more *favourable* publicity. And he wanted his English countrymen to come out in far greater numbers to see the country he had grown to value. He wanted them to come both as settlers and as tourists.

Lorne was the ideal promoter. Blond, fit and good-looking (his sister wrote of his "gracious character and beautiful exterior"), he was young – only thirty-three when he received his appointment in 1878 – and intelligent. He read widely, dabbled in most of the arts and wrote passable poetry. He had also married about as favourably as a young man of his day could; his wife was Louise, the fourth and most beautiful daughter of Queen Victoria. Princess Louise, as artistically inclined as her husband, painted and sculpted. She was an excellent conversationalist, in English or French, and at political and social occasions she managed to charm the stuffiest Orangeman or the most straight-laced *Bleu* from Quebec.

Lorne began his Canadian campaign modestly by writing to his friends, titled gentlemen and wealthy leaders, to prevail on them to visit Canada, but he was politely rebuffed. Canada didn't interest them. Then he appealed to the great newspapers of London for some attention. "I do not grudge the incessant praise [America] gets," he said in one letter to the *Times'* John Walter, "but why should our own 4,000,000 of people, who in proportion have made as much progress and are rapidly growing into a power, receive so little sympathy? . . . I have observed an unfortunate impression among Canadians," Lorne went on, "that your great paper has some antipathy to them and to the interests of their country." Walter didn't budge in his attitude to Canada and, like other English papers, refused to send a correspondent to report events in Ottawa.

the tour begins

Lorne decided on more direct action. In the summer of 1881, after months of pleas, cajolery and offers of hard cash, he persuaded four English reporters to accompany him, at his expense, on a tour across the country from Toronto all the way to the Rockies. One of the four was a writer named Austin from the *Times*. But his presence didn't indicate any capitulation on John Walter's part; Austin just happened to be a friend of Lorne's and just happened to be visiting the United States in the summer of 1881.

Canadian newspapers hardly concealed their

H.R.H. Louisa Carolina Alberta, the fourth and most beautiful daughter of Queen Victoria, married the Marquis of Lorne in 1871 and came to Canada with him seven years later. Her popularity with Canadians, especially Westerners, is evident in the name given to the new District of Alberta in 1882 and the rechristening by CPR surveyors of Emerald Lake as Lake Louise, jewel of the Rockies, near Banff Springs.

John Douglas Sutherland Campbell, Marquis of Lorne, whose father was heard to exclaim, "The Queen must be a very proud woman to have her daughter married to the son of the Duke of Argyll," took a keen interest in the developing cultural life of Canada. His support of the Royal Canadian Academy of Arts in 1880 extended to purchasing canvases by Watson and O'Brien for Windsor Castle, and he was instrumental in founding the Royal Society in 1882. Lorne's tour across the country to the Rocky Mountains inspired his paraphrase of Psalm 121, the hymn,
Unto the hills around do I lift up
My longing eyês.
and the more secular lines beginning
Away to the West, Westward Ho!
   Westward Ho!
Where over the prairies, the summer
   winds blow!

chagrin that they weren't included in the all-expense-paid junket. The Brockville *Recorder* called for a newspaper boycott of Lorne's activities, and only the Toronto *Globe* bothered to send along a reporter to cover the tour. Thus Lorne's party set off on its journey under a small black cloud. The atmosphere wasn't improved for the English press when the first 95-mile leg of the trip, from Toronto to Owen Sound by rail, took eleven hours. The slow pace was the result of what Austin of the *Times* called "the embarrassing eagerness of Canadians to deliver an address or two to the governor general." All along the line, at almost every village, hamlet and crossroads, Lorne was obliged to acknowledge words of welcome for himself and words of praise for his mother-in-law, Queen Victoria. The English reporters announced that they found the speechification nearly as wearing as Ontario's summer dust.

lavish praise

But that first day's grind was the last complaint anyone could honestly raise. The tour turned out a huge success. The English newspapermen were dazzled by the energy, variety and vastness of the Canadian scene. The clear waters of Lake Superior, the rugged Lakehead wilderness, the Indians, frontier Winnipeg, the steamer trip down the Saskatchewan, and the fabulous Rockies were a stunning delight to the newsmen. They wrote reams of copy, all of it lavish in its praise of Canada. On August 18, the mighty *Times* admitted error; in an editorial, it declared that Canada was not the barren land it had been led to believe, but was a thriving country, deserving of English attention and of English settlement. And later it echoed the words of Lorne when he told a meeting of the Manitoba Club in Winnipeg on October 18, "You have a country whose value it would be insanity to question."

THE MARQUIS
TOURS CANAD

Break-neck Steps in Quebec City, a favourite of artists.

the summer and fall of 1881, the Marquis
Lorne took an extensive cross-country
r to see for himself some of the natural
ources and the conditions of the country
was so energetically promoting to potential
migrants. He travelled from Halifax to
rtage La Prairie, the end-of-line, by train,
en, in horse-drawn wagons, and camping er.
te, crossed the prairies to the Rockies,
oming even more enthusiastic about the
ght prospects for settlers in a new land.

lifax, a port to which steamers from the Mersey sail.

es of sawn lumber, stacked on the banks of the Ottawa.

Governor General Lorne's tour inspired many
Old Country farmers and workers, who were
considering emigrating to the United States, to set
their sights for Canada instead. And it persuaded
English tourists to venture west at last, to see the
country the *Times* and the *Scotsman* were now
extolling. The peak year for visitors to Canada was
1885, but they came in considerable numbers in
each year of the decade during the travelling
season.

impressions of Canada

Some of them came specifically to report back
to newspaper editors, to potential settlers, to
organizations looking at Canada as a potential
convention site. In the wake of Lorne's tour,
serialized descriptions of cross-Canada journeys
appeared in dozens of English papers. Almost as
many scouts for settlement groups showed up, and
they, too, eventually published their impressions in
books and pamphlets filled with practical advice.

"Many young men of what is commonly called
the upper middle class," began the introduction to
Making A Start In Canada, by Professor Alfred
Church of London, "leave their country to seek
fortune, or to put the case more modestly, subsist-
ence, in Canada. It has occurred to me, having
recently sent two sons to that country, to publish
some extracts from the letters in which they have
described their experiences." The two Church lads,
both of them teenagers, turned out to be ideal
settlers. After working in several areas of the
country, they finally homesteaded near Calgary,
built a hut, "rather like a pig sty," and described
their Canadian situation as "quite jolly."

Montreal soon acquired a reputation as a
congenial location for a convention. The most
important, held in the summer of 1884, was a
conclave of the British Association for the Advancement of Science. It brought to Canada

*For its transcontinental timetable
of July 3, 1886, the CPR could boast
of "the longest continuous railway
in the world under one management."*

TRANSCONTINENTAL TRAVELLERS

After the excess of last-spike-driving in late 1885, the CPR was ready for transcontinental service. On June 26, 1886, Montreal crowds cheered the *Pacific Express* with coaches, colonist cars, sleeping and dining cars, as it headed out at 20:00 hours (the CPR had adopted Fleming's 24-hour time system) for Port Moody, B.C. It made the 2,900-mile journey in 139 hours, with many stops along the way. The elegant but heavy dining cars had to be side-lined before the train attempted the steep grades and sharp curves through the mountains. Company officials weren't on the train; they were busy planning accommodation and restaurant facilities for prospective tourists and a connecting trans-Pacific steamship service to provide a new route to the Orient.

The parlour car's elegant interior is painted in for this Notman composite of well-dressed travellers.

Gourmet travellers might be tempted by the antelope steak – a delicacy found only in Canada.

The eight-course meal offered on this 1886 menu cost 75¢, a "choice Havana cigar" 10¢ or 25¢.

118

This artist's sketch for the London Illustrated *might have deterred potential emigrants, although the colonists seem oblivious to the crowded conditions.*

When Buffalo Bill brought his Wild West Show to Montreal in 1885, he added battle scenes of the N.W. Rebellion to his act. Wm. Notman took this portrait of Cody with his star, Chief Sitting Bull.

distinguished scientists, philosophers and thinkers; so concerned was the Canadian government for the convention's success that it contributed $25,000 toward the delegates' expenses, dispatched cabinet ministers, including Sir John A. himself, to greet the visitors, and helped arrange a tour aboard a CPR train to the Rockies. They needn't have worried; the conventioners pronounced the gathering an intellectual and social triumph. When they returned home, they publicized their favourable, even glowing, opinions of Canada – opinions that did occasionally smack of a peculiarly English-upper-class snobbery. "I was struck all along," recorded Lady Clara Raleigh, wife of the Association's president, "with the far superior accent of the working man in Canada."

lecturers and tourists

Some English visitors, like Matthew Arnold, made Canada a stopping point on the international lecture circuit. In the winter of 1884, Arnold spoke to an Atheneum Club luncheon at the Windsor Hotel in Montreal, but his listeners, as it happened, didn't care for the talk, a presumptuous lecture on relations between English Canadians and French Canadians. "I said that the pretensions of the Catholic Church and the 'black' Presbyterians of the Protestants both hindered the fusion of French and English," Arnold wrote back to England. "Some of the Catholics much resented this; the Protestants took it better." Certainly poet Louis Fréchette had felt offended; he stomped out when Arnold called the Catholic Church "obsolete." None of this experience daunted Arnold; he liked Montreal. "I would sooner be a poor priest in Quebec," he wrote, "than a rich hog merchant in Chicago."

But most of the visitors were simply tourists. Some of them came to spend money, as though they'd embarked on a western version of the Grand

Tour. Others came for a holiday trip on the cheap. And like any tourists they often assumed they could "do" Canada in a breathtakingly brief time. Thomas Greenwood, an English businessman, writing of his travels through North America, called his book *A Tour In the States And Canada: Out And Home In Six Weeks.*

A set pattern of travel quickly evolved. It ran in a straight line, east to west. Tourists followed the line of the railroads, and along that route there developed, inevitably, a series of natural wonders and local celebrities that every visitor felt obliged to take in – Montmorency Falls, the Ice Palace and Victoria Bridge in Montreal; Jefferson Davis, the aging president of the Southern Confederacy, who spent some of his declining years in Montreal, frequently lounging in the bar of St. Lawrence Hall; the Parliamentary Library in Ottawa; the University of Toronto; the tavern on Toronto Island run by the world's champion oarsman, Ned Hanlan; Mrs. Janet Hanning, Thomas Carlyle's sister, who lived in Hamilton, Ontario; Niagara Falls; and, running west, the passenger steamers on the Great Lakes, Winnipeg, the Mounties, the great ranges of the North-West, the Rockies. . . .

likes and dislikes

From the wealth of sights and attractions, from their glimpses of everyday Canadian life, the tourists rapidly sorted out their likes and dislikes. Collectively, they demonstrated surprising unanimity. And frequently their views did not exactly square with the ways Canadians saw themselves.

To the British, Montreal was not quite the colourful cosmopolitan metropolis most Canadians imagined it to be. "Montreal is too French and idle-looking to be impressive," Lady Raleigh wrote. But Toronto seemed to bowl over everyone. "The good people of Toronto hold their heads higher than those in Montreal," announced Hugh

Fraser, an Inverness farmer. For the Scottish businessman, Hugh Bryce, Toronto was "of striking appearance," and for Charles Elliott, a Devonshire horse-breeder, it was "the most progressive city in Her Majesty's dominion."

But the city that drew the most ecstatic raves from Charles Elliott, a city that was "beautiful," with "elegant houses," "handsome churches," "good drainage" and "streets of noble dimensions," was none other than Hamilton, Ontario. To Elliott, even Hamilton's "Asylum at the summit of the mountain [was] a lovely sight, though somewhat marred by the thought of the poor creatures inside."

exotic or barbarous?

Niagara Falls, perhaps through exaggerated advertising, often disappointed tourists. "I complained to the landlord at the Prospect House," wrote a London architect named Thomas Rickman, "that there was less water than I had expected." But the Rockies and the British Columbia wilderness were a sensation for everyone. "The Fraser River is not only wonderful," reported George Bryce, an English doctor, "it is terrific in its grandeur."

Many customs and practices that Canadians took for granted struck their visitors as exotic or even barbarous. Sleigh rides ("On a clear and starry night, ten or twelve fun-loving spirits of both sexes embark on a lumber sleigh . . ."); Canadian teas ("It is likely to provide the consumer with nourishment for a week ensuing"); and local dialect ("The Canadian language is characterized by such as 'Well, sir,' 'I guess,' 'you bet' and 'is that so?' ") utterly charmed the English. But they could never grow accustomed to public eating habits. They deplored Canadian table manners and complained of the lack of style in serving food. "What can a man possibly do," John Rowan

John William Dawson
The Man Who Made McGill

Nova Scotia-born William Dawson became principal of McGill University in 1855 at thirty-five and almost single-handedly shaped its growth until his retirement in 1893. His first innovation was to offer courses in applied sciences, and throughout his tenure he promoted the inclusion of scientific studies in a still predominantly classical curriculum. He wrote many books in his own field of geology, including *The Origin of the World: The Story of the Earth and Man* (1872), and was a charter member of the Royal Society formed in 1882. An advocate of technological education for high school students moving into an increasingly industrialized society, he also championed higher education for women–a controversial issue of the time. Strangely enough he opposed mixed classes but succeeded in setting up, with the financial help of Donald Smith, separate classes for women at McGill in 1884. Coincidentally, that was also the year he was knighted.

asked, "with a dozen different dishes all at once before him?" And J.J. Ritchie wasn't certain whether he was watching democracy in action or simply a boorish display when he dined with Canadians. "It seemed strange," he wrote back to his English paper, "to sit at dinner and see great rough fellows, with the manners of ploughmen, quaffing costly champagne, and fancying themselves pictures of gentility and taste."

But two things at least made up for the rough manners: the prices were low and the hospitality was abundant and warm. For travellers accustomed to the European scale of costs, Canada seemed an immense bargain, and every visitor commented on the prices he paid. "At the Gravenhurst Hotel," recorded a Scottish tourist named Berry, "we got for one shilling each a dinner of three courses, a glass of beer and a drive to the railway in the hotel conveyance – with a cigar thrown in."

Even more gratifying to Berry and to all visitors like him was the warmth of their reception in Canada. "Canadian hospitality," Berry wrote, "can be compared in its heartiness and extent only with Highland or Irish." Canadians might well be the boors the *Times* once portrayed, the tourists seemed to agree, but that didn't count for much when at last they encountered Canadians at home. "Here," Hugh Bryce wrote admiringly, "I found civility and unbounded hospitality, persons exchanging the most pleasant salutations on meeting each other and ever ready to give neighbourly assistance in fencing a property, digging a well, or

any other necessary work."

What the tourists were *not* willing to concede, no matter how charming and distinctive in personality they found the people of Canada, was that Canadians were somehow forging a new, non-English nation of people. To them, Canadians were simply another variety of Englishman, not a unique species like the Americans. "The people have an English look," J.E. Ritchie, the journalist, argued. "Directly you pass the border into the States you see the difference. There is an astonishing contrast between the healthy Canadians and the lean and yellow Yankees."

The Yankees, for their part, disagreed. If the English were unable to grant Canadians a separate identity, the Americans couldn't help spotting a decided "Canadian type." "I had been told that the Canadians are second-hand Englishmen," wrote Charles Dudley Warner for *Harper's* magazine in 1889. "No estimate could convey a more erroneous impression. . . One can already mark with tolerable distinctiveness a Canadian type which is neither English nor American."

All of which left Canada with a fresh dilemma. At the beginning of the eighties, Mother England refused to take Canadians seriously and treated them lightly, as "colonists." By the end of the decade, England had at least learned to pay attention to Canadians and even to grant them a measure of respect and affection. But it still refused to take the next step in recognition – to accord to Canadians the distinction of being different from themselves.

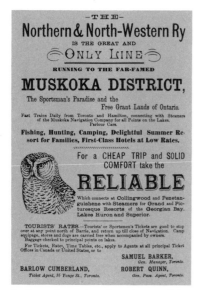
Railway lines other than the CPR did exist! In an 1886 tourist guidebook, the Northern & North-Western Railway promised "fast trains daily" running to the "far-famed Muskoka District."

Opposite page: *Experienced travellers, to judge from the baggage stickers, and obviously Scots; but perhaps the daughter is a musician (Is that a violin case?) who has come to Montreal to start her Canadian tour after performances in Paris and Dresden.*

ACKNOWLEDGEMENTS

While working on the chapter that deals with racism in the 1880s, I struck up a correspondence with Major J. S. Matthews of the Vancouver Archives. The Major took an interest in my project and, in letters and in precious copies of pamphlets he had himself written in earlier days, he offered me a thorough education in the anti-Oriental feeling around Vancouver over the last decades of the nineteenth century. Major Matthews, generous in his help and wise in his scholarship, was altogether typical of the people I encountered in libraries and through correspondence as I was researching the book.

Naturally I read books on the period, dozens and dozens of books–histories, memoirs, diaries, journals, travel accounts–all were enlightening, often funny, sometimes stylishly constructed, frequently ponderous, but always packed with nuggets of first-hand information. Then there were the newspapers which I read at the Central Library in Toronto. The library's curators and attendants were, like Major Matthews, patient and helpful, but there wasn't much they could do about the agony of reading newspapers reduced to microfilm.

Still, eye strain was a small price to pay for the adventure in self-education I might otherwise have missed, and I'm grateful to all the generous and dedicated people, beginning with Major Matthews, who showed me the way.

Jack Batten

Photo: Charlotte Sykes

The Author

Jack Batten practised law in Toronto, his home city, for four years before he realized that, as a lawyer, his future lay in writing. Since making the switch in professions, he has worked as a staff writer at *Maclean's* and *The Canadian*, as managing editor of *Saturday Night* and, after he began freelancing in 1968, he has been jazz columnist for the *Globe and Mail* and has written on various topics for magazines that range from *Chatelaine* to *Rolling Stone*. He has also written eight books, most recently *The Leafs in Autumn*.

INDEX

The page numbers in italics refer
to illustrations and captions

Agricultural colonies, 49, 54
Albani, Madame Emma, 94
Anglicans, 57, 113
Annapolis Valley, 87
Annexation, *8*, 38
Arnold, Matthew, 95, 120
Atlantic Monthly, 97

Bands, *32, 89, 98, 99*
Banks and banking, 26, 28, 84
Barkerville, *62*
Barnum, P. T., *31*, 113
Batoche, *46, 47*
Battleford, *14*, 38, 41-42, *43, 47*
Beaty, James, 72-73
Beecher, Henry Ward, 86
Beef, Joe, 29, *30*
Bell Farm, 56, *56*
Bell Telephone Company, *103*
Bengough, John Wilson, *38, 39, 108*
Big Bear, *36, 46*
Blacksmiths, 12
Blackwood's Magazine, 97
Blake, Edward, *39, 69, 70,* 71
Bone, P. Turner, *6, 8*, 15, 20
Book publishing and publishers, *93,*
    94, 96-98, *109, 110*
Bookshops, 96
Booth, General William, 86
Bootlegging, 20
Boston Bar, *18-19, 59*
Bowell, Mackenzie, 71
Brandon, 12, 40-41
Breakneck Steps (Quebec), 116
British America Ranch Company, 57
British Army, 87-88
British Association for the Advancement
    of Science, 117-20
British Columbia, 9, *11, 16,* 18-19,
    20, 21, 59-65, 121
Brown, George, *38, 39,* 40
Bryan, William Jennings, 86
Brymner, William, *34, 35*
Burdett-Coutts, Baroness, 56

Calgary, 8, 12, *14,* 15, *36,* 50, *57,* 117

Canada (ship), *82*
Canadian Pacific Railway, 20, 23,
    49, *52,* 56, *64, 65, 77, 112,* 113,
    115, 118, 120
    advertising and promotion, *9, 22,
    23,* 38, *49*
    building of, *6, 8, 8, 9, 11,*
    11-21, *12, 14, 15, 16, 17, 18, 19,
    26, 59, 59, 60, 60, 61,* 63, *104*
    in North-West Rebellion, *46*
Canadian Trades and Labor Congress,104
Cannington Manor, *48,* 49, *50, 51,* 56-57
Card, Charles, 55
Cardston, 55
Cariboo Trail, 18
Carling, John, 75-76, *76*
Carlton Trail, *40,* 50, *52*
Carlyle, Thomas, 121
Carman, Bliss, 83-84, *86,* 94, 95, 96
Carnivals, *24,* 25-27, 88, *89*
Cartoons, 8, *38, 39, 69, 74, 108*
Cartwright, Sir R. J., 73, 75, 76
Castors, 44
Cathcart, Lady Gordon, 56
Charity, 15, 28
Child labour, 102, 104
China painting, 85
Chinese, 7, 11, *18,* 18-19, 59-65,
    58, 59, 62, 63
Choate, Rufus, 82
Choirs, 93
Churches, 7, 13, 15, 28, 29, 44, 60,
    63, 84
Church, Alfred, 117
Churn, *78*
Clothes, 13, 32, 51, *51, 52,* 57, 88
Clubs, 13, 25, 32, *51,* 88, 116, 120
Coal, 87
Coal-oil lamps, 50, *78*
Coblentz brothers, 53, *53*
Cochrane, M. H. *57*
Cockneys, 53, 56
Cody, William F., *120*
Collins, William, 101, 104 107, 108
Colonization, 56
Concerts, *89,* 93, *98* 99
Conservative party, 44, 69-71,
    72-76, 84
Controverted Elections Act, 73
Co-operatives, 107
Craigellachie, 21
Crane, Matilda Maude, 85
Crawford, Isabella V. *94,* 95, *95*

Crémazie, Octave, *29*
Criminal Code, 55
Croats, 54
Crowfoot, 15, *15*
Cut Knife Hill, battle of, 43 *47*
Cutlery, 50
Cyr, Louis, 31, *31*
Czechs, 54

Dances and balls, 26, 49, 53, 57
Dartmouth, 88
Davin, Nicholas Flood, 37-38, *41*
Davis, Jefferson, 121
Dawson, Sir John William, 30, *121*
Deighton, Gassy Jack, 60
Denison, Lieut.-Col. Frederick, 114
De Sola, Clarence I., 20
Dewdney, Edgar, 11, *13,* 98
Diorama, *44*
Diseases, 32
Dishes, 50
Dock workers, *106*
Doctors, 12, 32, 37, 38
Dog trains, 13
Drought, 49
Drummond, George, 30
Duck Lake, 40, 43
Dufferin, Lord, 32
Dumont, Gabriel, *46*

East Lynne, 53
Edmonton, 38, 40, 50, *52*
Elections, *70,* 72-75, *74*
Electricity, 25, *25,* 26, 29, *78,* 88
Engineers, 8, 11
English immigrants, 49, *50,* 53
Entertaining, *27,* 31-32, 53, 57, 72
Esterhazy, 54
Etiquette, 32
Experimental Farms system, *76*

Fabre, Bishop, 43
Factories, 8, 18, 27, 104, 107, 108
Fairs, *9,* 53, *101*
Family Herald, 50
Family life, 28, 50-53
Farming, 49, *49,* 50, *50,* 53, 54, 56,
    57, 81, 87, 96, *106*
Fashions, 13, 32, *51, 57, 88*
Fielding, William, 7
Fire escape, *78*
Fires, 15, 32, 60-63, *61,* 64, *78*
    84, *102,* 108

Fish Creek, *46*
Fishing industry, *106*
Fleming, Sandford, *12,* 18, 19, *104, 109*
Food, 27, 31-32, 50, 51, 103, *118,* 121
Food-gathering, 51
Fort Carlton, *46*
Fort Macleod, 40, 55
Fort William, 12
Foster, Captain William Joe, 81-82
Fraser, John, *90,* 94
Fraser River, *18,* 18-19, *60,* 121
Fraternal societies, 13-15, 84
Fréchette, Louis-Honoré, *29,* 120
Fredericton, 83, *86,* 93, 95
Frog Lake massacre, 43
Furniture, 50, *78,* 103
Fur trade, 59

Galt, Sir Alexander Tilloch,
    53-54, 113
Gas lamps, *78,* 88
Gastown (Vancouver), 60
Gerrymandering, 73-75
Ginger ale, *107*
Gooderham family, 75
Grand Trunk Railway, 25
Grant, George Monro, *109, 110*
Granville (Vancouver), 60, *61*
Grasshoppers, 49
Greenwood, Thomas, 121
Greeting cards, *30*
Grip, 38, 39, 108

Halifax, 8, 82, *84,* 85-88, *89,* 97
    106, 115, *117*
Hamilton, *32,* 101, 102, 121
Hanlan, Ned, 9, 121
Hanning, Janet, 121
Harness makers, 12
Harper's Magazine, 56, 97, 122
Harris, Robert, *34, 35*
Harvesters, 13
Harvey, George, 85, *87*
Head tax, on Chinese, 63
Heinrich, Max, 99
Herbs, 51-53
Herchmer, Superintendent, 43, 55
High River, *72*
Hirsch, 54
Holidays, 81, 88, 98, *99*
Holt City (Lake Louise), 19-20
Holt, Tim, *6,* 19
Hospitals, 31, 32

Hotels
    Banff Springs, *112, 115*
    Fredericton, 95
    Montreal, 25, 29, *31,* 120, 121
    Ontario, 9, 121, 122
    Prairies, 12, 13, *14,* 38, 53
    Vancouver, 59, 60, 63, 64, 65
    Victoria, *73*
Hours of work, 103-4, 107
Household conveniences, *78*
House of Commons, *39,* 69
Houses, 8, 12, *26,* 27, *27,* 28, 29,
    30, 31, 50, 103
Howland, Mayor William, 107
Hudson's Bay Company, 11, 12, 13, *26*
Hungarians, 8, 53, 54

Ice Palace (Montreal), *24,* 26, 121
Illecillewaet River, *17*
*Illustrated Atlas of the Dominion of
Canada, 26*
Illustrated London News, 97, *112, 119*
Immigrants and immigration, 7, *7,* 8,
    9, 11, *22,* 28, 49, *50,* 53-57,
    59-65, *116,* 117, *119*
Indians, 15, *15,* 21, 40, 41, 43, *45, 46,* 63
    116
Intercolonial Railway, *83,* 87
Irish and Irish Canadians, 8, 28, 84
Irvine, Lieut.-Col. A. G., 19

Jackfish Bay, 21
Jews, 7, 20, *53,* 53-54
John McLeod (sailing ship), 83
Judge's Cut, *16*
Julien, Henri, *74*

Keefers station, *58, 59*
Kicking Horse Pass, *6,* 15, 19
Kinsey, Amos, *48*
Kirkpatrick, George, *69*
Kitchenware, 50
Knights of Labor, 101-108

Labour, 8, 11, 27, 29, 101-108
Lacombe, Albert, 15
Lake Louise, 20, *115*
Lake Superior, *11,* 15, *16,* 21, 116
Lampman, Archibald, 93, 94, *94,* 95, 96
Land-clearing, *106*
Land speculation, 8, 11-12, 13, *13,* 49
Laurie, Patrick Gammie, 38, 41-43, *43*
Laurier, Wilfrid, 44

Lavallée, Calixa, 93, 94, 98 *98*
Lavigne, Arthur, 98
Lectures, 83, 86-87, 107, 120
Leduc, Ozias, *34*
Lehmann, Lilli, 99
Lethbridge, 55
Liberal party, *29, 39,* 43, 44, 69,
    70, 71, 72-76, 84
Libraries, 107, 121
Lighthall, William Douw, 96, 97
Lighting, 50, *78*
Liquor, 7. 9, 13, 20, 31, 60, 63,
    64, 70, *71, 72, 73,* 75-76, *76,*
    102, 103, 107, 114, 115
Literature, 7, *29,* 37, 38, 83, *86,*
    90, 93, 94-95, *94,* 95-98, *97*
London, Ont., *34,* 69, 76, 104
Lorne, Marquis of, 7, 75, 93, 94,
    109, 110, 113, *113,* 115-17, *116*
Louise, Princess, Marchioness of
    Lorne, 93, *110,* 115, *115*
Lucas, Locksley, 59, 64, 65
Lumbering, *105, 106,* 117
Lytton, 18, 19, *59*

Macdonald, Sir John A.,
    7, 9, 11, *26,* 37, 38, *39,* 41, 44,
    46, 55, 63, 64, *69,* 70, 71, 73-75,
    76, 98, 101, 104, 120
Macdonald Tobacco Company, 27, *66*
McGibbon, Robert, 25
McGill University, 25, 30, *121*
Mackenzie, Alexander, *39,* 73
McKiernan, Charles, 29, *30*
McLaughlin, John J., *107*
Maclean, Mayor Malcolm, *61,* 63, 64
McLeod, Captain John, 83
Macoun, John, 12, *12,* 15
Magazines, 53, 97, 98
Manitoba, 7, 12-15, 49-54, 102
Maritimes, 9, 81-88, 102
Massey Manufacturing Company, 13
Mechanics' Institutes, 83, 107
Melita Trail, 50
Mercier, Honoré, 7, 44
Meredith, W. R., 69-70
Methodist Book and Publishing House,
    93, 96, 97
Métis, *15,* 21, 37, *46*
Middleton, Maj.-Gen. Frederick, *46, 47*
Militia, 26, 32, *32,* 43-44, *46,* 85, 107
Mining, 59-60, *81*
Minstrel shows, *85,* 86

Montmorency Falls, 121
Montreal, 8, 11, 21, *23, 24, 25,*
    25-32, 26, 28, *28,* 29, *30, 31, 32,*
    43, 97, 104, 107, 117, *118,* 120,
    121, *122*
Montreal & Western Land Company, 56
Moose Jaw, 50
Moosomin, *50,* 56
Mormons, 53, 54-55, *55,* 56
Mowat, Oliver, 69, 70, *70,* 104
Music, 25, 53, 69, 83, 84, *84,* 85,
    86, 93, *93,* 94, 98, *98*

National Gallery, *91,* 94
Nationalism, 95-96
National Policy, *39,* 101
Navvies, *6,* 11, 15, *16, 17,* 18,
    19-20, 59-65, *60, 63*
Nepigon Bay and River, *11, 17*
New Brunswick, 82-85, 96
Newspapers and journalists
    B.C., 60, 63, 64
    British, 109, 113, 115-16, 117, 122
    Maritimes, 84, 85, 87, 88
    Montreal, *38,* 44, 45
    Ontario, 7, 8, 38, 69, 71, 75,
    103, 114, 116
    Prairies, 8, *36,* 37, *37,* 38-43,
    40, 41, 43, 53, 55
News-stands, 97
New Westminster, 65, *65*
Niagara Falls, 121
Nile Expedition, 113-15, *114*
Northern & North-Western Railway, *122*
North-West Mounted Police, 12, *14,*
    15, *15,* 19, 20-21, 43, *46,* 55, 57,
    64, 65, 121
North-West Rebellion, 15, 21, *36,* 40,
    41-44, *42, 43, 44, 46,* 56, 85, *120*
North-West Territories, 11-12, *13,*
    15, 49-57, 98
Nor'West Farmer, 53
Notman photographic studios,
    90, 94, *118-19, 120*
Nova Scotia, 7, *78,* 81-88, 95

O'Brien, Lucius, *90, 91,* 94, *109,*
    110, 116
"O Canada," 98, *98*
Odd Fellows, 13
Office buildings, 29
O'Keefe family, 75
Old North Trail, 50

Oliver, Frank, *37,* 38, 40, *40*
Onderdonk, Andrew, *11, 17, 18,*
    18-19, 59, *59,* 60, *60,* 63, *63*
Ontario, 15-18, 28, 69-76
Opera, 69, *85,* 86, 98
Oppenheimer, Mayor David, *61*
Orange Order, 15, 71, 72
Oratorio, 98
Orchestras and bands, 69, 84, 85,
    86, 93, 98, 99
Orquell (clipper ship), 81-82
Osler, Britton Bath, *42*
Ottawa, 32, 71, 72, 94, 96, 104, 114
Ottawa Valley, 96, *105, 117*
Otter, Lieut.-Col. William, 43
Our Deportment, 32
Ox-carts, 13, 38, 40

Pacific Scandal, 26
Painting, *34,* 85, 87, *90-91, 109, 116*
Parks, *61, 112*
Parliament Buildings, *114,* 121
Patronage, 70
Pedlars, *108*
Peel, Paul, *34*
Perambulator, *78*
Peruvian, S.S., 8
Phillips-Wolley, Sir Clive, 97
Photography, 12, *90,* 94, *118-19, 120*
Picnics, *55,* 70, 103
Picturesque Canada, 109, 110
Picturesque Montreal, 29
Pierce, Captain E.M., 49, *50,* 56-57
Pile of Bones (Regina), 11-12, *13*
Plasterers' Union, 108
Plumbing, *78*
Pocock, Roger, 97
Police, *31, 32,* 63, 64, 65, 87, 107
    See also North-West Mounted Police
Politics, 69-76
Population, *14, 54,* 83
Port Moody, 21, 60, 63, *118*
Poundmaker, *15,* 43, *45, 46*
Prairies, 11-15, 38, 41, 49, *116*
Presbyterians, 13, 63, *70,* 87, *109,* 120
Prices, 12, *31,* 50, 51, 60, 94, 97,
    102-103, *118-19,* 122
Primitive Methodist Colony, 56
Prince Albert, *14,* 40
Prince Edward Island, 81, 83
Printing presses, 38, 40
Protestants, 28, *39,* 120

Qu'Appelle Valley, *52*
Quebec, 7, 9
Quebec City, 93, 98, *99, 116*
Queen's University, *104, 109*

Racial bigotry, 7, 59
Railways, *104, 121, 122*
    See also under company names
Ranching, *57*
Raycroft, Superintendent, 64, 65
Redpath, Peter, 30
Red River cart, *48*
Refrigeration, *78, 106*
Regina, 12, 37, 38, *41, 42,* 98
Reid, George A., *34, 35*
Religious bigotry, 7
Remittance men, 49, 57
Richardson, Hugh, *42*
Riel, Louis, 21, 32, 37, *39, 42,* 43,
    43, 44, *45, 46, 47,* 56, 85
Riots, 20, 32
Road-building, *101, 106*
Robert Kerr (barque), 60
Roberts, Charles, G. D., 83, *86, 90,*
    93, 94-95, 96
Rocky Mountains, 8, 9, 15, 19, 21,
    112, 115, 116, 120, 121
Rogers Pass, *16, 17*
Roman Catholics, 8, 28, *29, 39,* 44,
    46, 120
Roper, Edward, *65*
Rose Belford's Canadian Monthly, 98
Royal Canadian Academy of Arts, *34,*
    35, 87, 90, 91, 94, *110, 116*
Royal Commission on the Relations of
    Labor and Capital, 27, 101, 103,
    104, 108
Royal Navy, 86, 87, 88
Royal Society, 94, *109, 116, 121*
Ryerson, Egerton, *93*

Sailing ships, 9, 60, 81-83, *82*
St. Andrews Ward (Toronto), 102-3
Saint John, 82, 83, 84-85
Salaries, 29, 76
Saloons, 7, 13, *14,* 29, *30,* 59, 60, 63,
    72, 76, *77,* 87, 107, 121
Sandham, Henry, *90*
Sanitation, *78*
Saskatchewan River, 43, 116
Saskatoon, 51, 56
Saturday Night, 97
Sawmills, 63

Schell, Fred, *110*
Schools, *52,* 57, 70
Science, 94, *121*
Scots and Scottish Canadians, 8,
    29-30, 44, *72,* 81, 84, *122*
Scott, Duncan Campbell, 95
Scribner's Monthly, 97
Secret ballot, 74
Senator (steamer), *61*
Separatism, 7
Serbians, 54
Settlement, *36,* 49, *49,* 50, *52,*
    53-57
Sewing machine, *78*
Sherbrooke, 9
Ship-building, 83
Sitting Bull, 120
Skuzzy (paddlewheeler), *18,* 18-19
Slovaks, 54
Smith, Donald A., 21, *26,* 27, *27,* 30-31,*121*
Smith, Frank, 107
Smith, Goldwin, 94, 95
Sod houses, 50
Soft drinks, *107*
Songs, 53, 98
Sports and games, *31, 32,* 38, *60,*
    84, 89
    baseball, 32, 88
    boxing, 84-85
    cricket, 32, 49, 57, 88
    football, 32, 57, 88
    hockey, 25, 88
    horseracing, *51*
    hunting, 49, 51, *51,* 53, *57, 78*
    lacrosse, 25, 32, *110*
    regattas, 81, 88
    riding, *88*
    rowing, 9, *111*
    skating, 25, 26, *110*
    sleighing, 8, 25-26, 121
    snowshoeing, 8, 25, 26
    tennis, 32, 49, 88, *88*
    tobogganing, 8, 26, 32
Standard time, *104*
Stanley, Lord, *61*
Steamers, 9, *18,* 18-19, 40, *61,* 64,
    65, 81, 82, *117, 118,* 121
Steele, Inspector Sam, 20-21
Stephen, George, 11, *22, 26, 27,*
    30-31, 113
Stewart, Chief John, 64
Stoves, 50
Street railways, 28, 107

Strikes, 8, 20-21, 29, 63, 107-108
Sullivan, John L., 84-85
Sumner Colony, 53

Telegraph, 38
Telephones, 88, *103*
Temperance Colony, 56
Temperance movement, 41, 53, 56, 76,
    96, 102
Textile industry, 28
Theatre, 83, *85,* 85-86
Theatrical parties, 32
Tilley, Sir Samuel Leonard, *71*
Timber resources, 70
Tobacco, *21,* 27, 28, *66, 72, 104, 118*
Toronto, 7, 8, 9, *32,* 72, 93, 95,
    97, 98, 99, 102-103, 104, 107,
    111, 115, 121
Toronto Industrial Exhibition, *101*
Toronto Street Railway, 107
Tourists, 88, 117, 120-22
Trade, *82*
Trades and Labor Congress, 108
Trinity College (Toronto), 93, *94*
Trudel, F. X. A., 44
Tupper, Sir Charles, 76
Twain, Mark, 25, 29
Typewriter, *78*

Unemployment, 83
Union Jack, 69, 81
United Fruit Company, 83
Universities, 25, *29,* 30, 83, *86,*
    94, *104, 109,* 121
University of New Brunswick, 83, *86,* 94
University of Toronto, 121

Vaccination, 32
Vancouver, 11, 15, 21, 59-65, *61,*
    62, 64, 77, 98
Van Horne, William, 11, 15, 19, *19,*
    21, *21,* 60, *61, 112*
Vass, Julian, 54
Vaudeville, *85*
Vézina, Joseph, 98
Victoria, *62, 63,* 64, 65, *73, 77, 102*
Victoria, Queen, 113, 116

Wages, 27, 29, 63, 101-108
Walker, Horatio, *90,* 94
Warner, Charles Dudley, 56, 122
Washing machine, *78*
Watson, Homer, *90, 91,* 94, *116*

Week, The, 72, 94, 95, 97
Wheat, 13
White, Thomas, 71
Wilde, Oscar, 87, 94, 95
Winnipeg, 8, 12-15, 38, 40, 50, 53,
    54, *102,* 116, 121
Wolseley, Sir Garnet, 114, *114*
Women, higher education for, *121*
Working conditions, 102
W. R. Grace Company, 83

Yale, B.C., *11, 17,* 60, *60*
York boats, 40
York Farmers Colonization Co., 56
Young, Chief Justice Sir William, 88

PICTURE CREDITS

We would like to acknowledge the help and cooperation of the directors and staff of the various public institutions and the private firms and individuals who made available paintings, posters, mementoes, collections and albums as well as photographs and gave us permission to reproduce them. Every effort has been made to identify and credit appropriately the sources of all illustrations used in this book. Any further information will be appreciated and acknowledged in subsequent editions.

The illustrations are listed in the order of their appearance on the page, left to right, top to bottom. Principal sources are credited under these abbreviations:

CIN — *Canadian Illustrated News*
CP — Corporate Archives, Canadian Pacific
GA — Glenbow-Alberta Institute
ILN — *Illustrated London News*
MTCL — Metropolitan Toronto Central Library
NG — National Gallery of Canada, Ottawa
NPA — Notman Photographic Archives
OA — Ontario Archives
PABC — Provincial Archives, Victoria, B.C.
PAC — Public Archives of Canada
PANS — Public Archives of Nova Scotia
VHR — *Van Horne's Road*, Omer Lavallée, Montreal, Railfare Enterprises Ltd.

/1 ILN, Titus Gallery, Victoria, B.C. /2 GA /4 Eaton's of Canada Archives /6 PABC /7 VHR /8 *Diogenes* /9 VHR /10 PABC /11 CP /12 Private Collection /13 OA, Osler File /14 GA; CP, photograph by Boorne & May /15 Archives Nationales du Québec /16 CP; PABC; CP /17 CP; PABC; PABC; CP /18 Vancouver Public Library /19 PAC, C 8549 /20 VHR /21 Private Collection /22 CP; CP /23 VHR; CP; CP /24 McCord Museum, Montreal /25 Brosseau Scrapbook /26 NPA; NPA /27 NPA; NPA; Brosseau Scrapbook /28 Canada Wide /29 Archives Nationales du Québec /30 Brosseau Scrapbook; *Montreal Gazette* /31 Brosseau Scrapbook; Roy Mitchell Photography /32 Brosseau Scrapbook /33 McCord Museum, Montreal /34 NG /35 From the collection of the Art Gallery of Hamilton, Ontario; NG; NG /36 *Calgary Herald* /37 Stanley A. Williams /38 *Grip* /39 All from *Grip*, MTCL /40 GA /41 OA;

Calgary Herald /42 GA; OA; OA /43 Fort Battleford National Historic Park /44 OA /45 GA /46 GA /47 PAC /48 Saskatchewan Archives /49 CP /50 Saskatchewan Archives /51 Saskatchewan Archives /52 Saskatchewan Archives; PAC C 3862 /53 Provincial Archives of Manitoba /54 GA /55 GA /56 Saskatchewan Archives /57 Private Collection; GA /58 PABC /59 VHR /60 PABC /61 City of Vancouver Public Archives; City of Vancouver Public Archives; NPA /62 PABC; PABC; City of Vancouver Public Archives /63 VHR /64 Vancouver Public Library /65 PAC /66-67 Macdonald Tobacco Company; All others MTCL, Pat Rogal, Fine Arts Department /68 MTCL /69 Brosseau Scrapbook /70 OA /71 *Grip*, MTCL /72 GA; GA; GA; *Calgary Herald* /73 PABC; Private Collection /74 *Canadian Illustrated News;* OA /75 OA /76 OA /77 PABC /78 *Domestic Life in Nineteenth Century Canada; Friendly Persuasion; Domestic Life in Nineteenth Century Canada;* OA; *Grip* /79 Fenelon Falls Historical Society; CIN; *Grip; Grip;* MTCL /80 R.E. Merrick, A.V. Services /81 *The Globe* /82 PANS /83 *The Globe* /84 Dalhousie University Archives, Killam Memorial Library, Halifax, N.S.; PANS /85 PANS; PANS /86 Dalhousie University, Halifax, N.S., William Inglis Morse Collection, Killam Memorial Library /87 PANS /88 PANS /89 Province House, Halifax, N.S. /90 From the collection of the Art Gallery of Hamilton, Ontario /91 NG; NG /92 McGraw-Hill Ryerson Limited, photographer Norman Mansfield /93 Brosseau Scrapbook /94 MTCL /95 University of Toronto Library /96 Private Collection /97 Coles Canadiana Collection /98 Editeur officiel du Québec /99 Archives Nationales du Québec /100 Fenelon Falls Museum /101 MTCL /102 Stovel Advocate Collection; PABC /103 OA /104 PAC C 14128 /105 Private collection /106 Fenelon Falls Museum; OA; Nova Scotia Museum; PAC /107 Canada Dry /108 *Grip;* PAC /109 *Picturesque Canada;* PAC C 23562 /110-111 All from *Picturesque Canada*, Titus Gallery, Victoria, B.C. /112 ILN, Titus Gallery Victoria, B.C. /113 *Canadian Life and Scenery*, private collection /114 Archives Nationales du Québec; NPA /115 *Harper's New Monthly Magazine* /116 Fenelon Falls Historical Society /116-117 *Canada Life and Scenery*, private collection /117 VHR /118 NPA; GA; VHR /119 ILN, Titus Gallery, Victoria, B.C. /120 NPA /121 PAC C 21617 /122 *Muskoka and the Northern Lakes of Canada*, Hunter Rose, Toronto /123 NPA /128 OA

1885

Métis form a provisional government with Louis Riel as president.

Rising of Métis and Indians in the North-West under the leadership of Riel; troops mobilized and sent to the North-West under General Middleton; engagements at Cut Knife Hill, Fish Creek, Duck Lake, Frog Lake, Batoche; surrender of Riel and Poundmaker; suppression of the revolt.

Trial and hanging of Riel; agitation in Quebec against the Dominion government's policy.

Donald Smith drives last spike in CPR at Craigellachie, Nov. 7.

CPR telegraph completed from Atlantic to Pacific.

The Dominion government imposes a tax on Chinese entering Canada.

General Statistics Act passed; *Statistical Year Book* instituted in 1886 on official basis.

Single-pole electric trolley demonstrated for first time at Toronto.

Universal Time System adopted at Greenwich, England; (Sir) Sandford Fleming acknowledged as the initiator of the movement for reform in time-reckoning.

1886

Sir John and Lady Macdonald travel to Pacific Coast by CPR.

Premier Fielding of Nova Scotia introduces a resolution asking an end to Confederation.

Debate in Parliament over execution of Riel.

Dominion Experimental Farms established at Ottawa by Agriculture Minister John Carling, with William Saunders as director.

Vancouver incorporated as city; fire on June 13 almost destroys city; 50 lives lost.

Archbishop Taschereau of Quebec becomes first Canadian Cardinal of Roman Catholic Church.

U.S. seizes Canadian sealing vessels in Bering Sea; dispute arises over jurisdiction; final settlement in 1898.

Charles G.D. Roberts publishes *In Divers Tones*.

Winnipeg Rowing Club incorporated.

Electric lights first used in St. John's, Newfoundland.

Conservatives appoint Royal Commission on the Relations of Labor and Capital.

1887

Macdonald's Conservatives retain power in the Dominion elections.

Wilfrid Laurier succeeds Edward Blake as leader of the Liberals.

First Interprovincial Conference of premiers held at Quebec City; they endorse reciprocity with U.S.

U.S. passes Fisheries Retaliation Act against Canada.

Vancouver loses its city charter over riots against Chinese labour.

Louis Fréchette publishes *La légende d'un peuple*.

CPR enters into contract with the Elder Company to place three steamers in the trans-Pacific service.

First electric street-railway system in Canada is opened in St. Catharines.